Learning Selenium Testing Tools

Third Edition

Leverage the power of Selenium to build your own real-time test cases from scratch

Raghavendra Prasad MG

PUBLISHING

BIRMINGHAM - MUMBAI

Learning Selenium Testing Tools
Third Edition

First published: November 2010

Second edition: October 2012

Third edition: February 2015

Production reference: 1180215

Published by Packt Publishing Ltd.
Livery Place
35 Livery Street
Birmingham B3 2PB, UK.

ISBN 978-1-78439-649-7

www.packtpub.com

Credits

Author
Raghavendra Prasad MG

Reviewers
Tarun Kumar Bhadauria
Viacheslav Klevchenia
Sreenath Sasikumar

Commissioning Editor
Pramila Balan

Acquisition Editor
Larissa Pinto

Content Development Editor
Melita Lobo

Technical Editor
Parag Topre

Copy Editors
Janbal Dharmaraj
Relin Hedly

Project Coordinator
Sanchita Mandal

Proofreaders
Simran Bhogal
Steve Maguire
Kevin McGowan

Indexer
Tejal Soni

Graphics
Sheetal Aute
Valentina D'silva
Disha Haria

Production Coordinator
Aparna Bhagat

Cover Work
Aparna Bhagat

About the Author

Raghavendra Prasad MG is basically an electronics and communication engineer from the University of Mysore and did his MBA from VMU. He is currently working as an automation architect and a QA lead at Riversand Global Technologies. He has been into test automation for more than 8 years. He is an automation tools and automation framework design trainer as well. He has trained at least 500 professionals so far. In his past experience, he worked as a corporate trainer on automation tools and automation framework design.

His previous experiences include Life Technologies (now Thermo Fischer Scientific Company), GT Nexus Software, MphasiS (an HP Company), Thomson-Reuters Inc., Telelogic (now IBM-Rational), Aztecsoft (now Mindtree Consulting Ltd), and many more.

He worked as a freelancer for automation and automation framework implementation.

He implemented various automation frameworks for more than 30 projects, starting from zero level on applications of multiple domains such as, ERP, CRM, ELM, financial domain, automobile, insurance and pension (on legacy systems), healthcare, biotechnology, cloud supply chain platform, and Master Data Management (MDM).

Raghu is especially well known for enabling the manual (or functional) tester towards automation. His experience in this area has become a key point for this book. Raghu has built his own tools on API automation, BI automation, and performance.

Raghu won an award for being the best performer in the keyword test automation framework design and implementation at GTNexus. He also won an Individual Summit award for Data Driven Test Automation Framework design and implementation at MphasiS, an HP Company for GM (General Motors, a supply chain project).

Raghu won an Excellence in Execution award at Telelogic, an IBM Company. He is passionate about test automation. You can reach him at his LinkedIn account, `https://in.linkedin.com/pub/raghavendra-prasad-mg/4/538/264`.

About the Reviewers

Tarun Kumar Bhadauria has been working in the field of software testing for about 8 years. He has worked on a gamut of software testing areas, that is, manual testing, automated UI testing, and performance testing. He has always had a penchant for Selenium and has been using it for the past 4 years. He is also the coauthor of the official Selenium document available at the Selenium headquarters. He is currently working at Zalando as a quality engineer.

Viacheslav Klevchenia studied at KPI, specializing in applied physics. Since 2008, he has been working in the field of QA and testing, and is engaged in automation testing of websites since 2012. Previously, he was interested in literature as a hobby, and now, he is currently keen in the field of public review of technical documentation (user manuals, specifications, and many more).

I would like to express my gratitude to the staff at Packt Publishing, who invited me to participate in the review of this publication.

Sreenath Sasikumar is currently a self-employed software professional and consultant working on open source projects. He specializes in automation testing and web application security. He is an active member of OWASP and also a volunteer at Mozilla Firefox.

He worked for IBM, QBurst, and DBG, helping small and enterprise clients with their automation and security needs.

He supports OWASP and initiated the official Google+ community of OWASP and also contributes to its projects. He is also the owner of the largest software testing community in Google+.

He has created eight Mozilla add-ons, one of which, Clear Console, was listed as the best add-on of the month in March 2013. It was also selected as one of the best Mozilla add-ons of the year in 2013. With a user base of more than 38,000, it has registered more than 525,000 downloads to date. He has also created the world's first, one-of-a-kind security testing browser bundle, PenQ.

Sreenath is also a regular speaker at technology events. In addition to webinars, he has also been a speaker at Google DevFest, Technopark GTech Conference, Coffee at DBG, Unicom Testing Conference, and many more.

www.PacktPub.com

Support files, eBooks, discount offers, and more

For support files and downloads related to your book, please visit www.PacktPub.com.

Did you know that Packt offers eBook versions of every book published, with PDF and ePub files available? You can upgrade to the eBook version at www.PacktPub.com and as a print book customer, you are entitled to a discount on the eBook copy. Get in touch with us at service@packtpub.com for more details.

At www.PacktPub.com, you can also read a collection of free technical articles, sign up for a range of free newsletters and receive exclusive discounts and offers on Packt books and eBooks.

https://www2.packtpub.com/books/subscription/packtlib

Do you need instant solutions to your IT questions? PacktLib is Packt's online digital book library. Here, you can search, access, and read Packt's entire library of books.

Why subscribe?
- Fully searchable across every book published by Packt
- Copy and paste, print, and bookmark content
- On demand and accessible via a web browser

Free access for Packt account holders

If you have an account with Packt at www.PacktPub.com, you can use this to access PacktLib today and view 9 entirely free books. Simply use your login credentials for immediate access.

To my ever loving parents, my beloved wife Manasa, my children Aishu and Chintu for giving me your full support to finish this book on time!
I love you all

Table of Contents

Preface

Selenium WebDriver is the most used automation tool for web-based applications. This book shows beginners, developers, and testers how to create automated test cases using Selenium. You will be able to use Selenium IDE for quick throwaway tests and you will learn to use Selenium WebDriver along with the automation framework development.

You will learn how to use Selenium WebDriver with both desktop browsers and mobile browsers as well learn good design patterns to ensure your tests will be extremely maintainable.

We have provided prerequisites as well, so that you are well versed with the topics needed to understand testing with Selenium. You will therefore not have to refer to other external sources to understand these topics.

What this book covers

Chapter 1, Getting Started with Selenium IDE, explains how to install Selenium IDE and record our first tests. We will see what is needed to work against AJAX applications.

Chapter 2, Locators, shows how we can find elements on the page to be used in our tests. We will use XPath, CSS, link text, and ID to find elements on the page so that we can interact with them.

Chapter 3, Overview of the Selenium WebDriver, discusses all the history and architectural designs for Selenium WebDriver. You will also go through the necessary items for setting up a development environment.

Chapter 4, Finding Elements, explains all the different techniques in searching elements using Selenium WebDriver. This chapter builds on the locators that we learned in *Chapter 2, Locators.*

Chapter 5, Design Patterns, introduces the different design patterns that can be used with Selenium WebDriver. The design patterns will show you how to make your tests more maintainable and allow more people to work on your code.

Chapter 6, Working with WebDriver, introduces all the different aspects of getting different browsers that Selenium WebDriver supports on desktop operating systems.

Chapter 7, Automation Framework Development and Building Utilities, explains the various types of automation frameworks and how to build the Hybrid automation framework with the design, architecture, and implementation. We are giving a plug and play Hybrid automation framework for Selenium WebDriver with the code bundle of this book.

Chapter 8, Mobile Devices, explains how Selenium WebDriver works on mobile devices to test mobile websites or sites built with responsive web design.

Chapter 9, Getting Started with the Selenium Grid, shows us how we can set up our Selenium Grid. We will also take a look at running tests in parallel to try bringing down the time it takes to run tests.

Chapter 10, Advanced User Interactions, explains how to build chains of actions together to help when you need to drag and drop or have key combinations working. We will also look at how we can press a mouse button and hold it down while we move the mouse.

Chapter 11, Working with HTML5, explains working with some of the HTML5 technologies that are becoming available to browsers. The Selenium WebDriver APIs are very similar to the JavaScript APIs in the browser in order to make use of them easier.

Chapter 12, Advanced Topics, explains how to capture network traffic between the browser and the web server. We finish off by capturing screenshots.

Chapter 13, Migrating from Remote Control to WebDriver, introduces how the interaction with the browser has changed and how we can convert our Selenium 1 tests to Selenium 2 to take advantage of the changes in Selenium WebDriver.

Appendix A, Automation Prerequisites for Selenium Automation, deals with the basics of Java and prerequisites related to programming, which is mandatorily required for automation testing. We are giving an automation prerequisites-related program of examples with this book.

Appendix B, Answers for Self-test Questions, has the answers to all the self-test questions in the previous chapters.

What you need for this book

- Mozilla Firefox
- Google Chrome
- Internet Explorer
- Opera
- Eclipse or IntelliJ IDEA
- Firebug
- Firefinder
- Xpath finder / XPath viewer (Firefox add-ons)
- Selenium IDE
- Selenium Grid
- Ubuntu Linux

Who this book is for

If you are a software quality assurance professional, software project manager, or a software developer interested in automated testing using Selenium, this book is for you. Web-based application developers will also benefit from this book.

Conventions

In this book, you will find a number of text styles that distinguish between different kinds of information. Here are some examples of these styles and an explanation of their meaning.

Code words in text, database table names, folder names, filenames, file extensions, pathnames, dummy URLs, user input, and Twitter handles are shown as follows: "If an item fails, then it will have an [error] entry."

A block of code is set as follows:

```
@Test
public void shouldCheckButtonOnChapter2Page(){
selenium.get("http://book.theautomatedtester.co.uk");
selenium.findElement(By.linkText("Chapter2")).click();
Assert.assertEquals(selenium.findElements(By.id("but1")).size(), 1);
}
```

When we wish to draw your attention to a particular part of a code block, the relevant lines or items are set in bold:

```
adb -s <serialId> forward tcp:8080 tcp:8080
```

Any command-line input or output is written as follows:

```
db shell am start -a android.intent.action.MAIN -n
```

New terms and **important words** are shown in bold. Words that you see on the screen, for example, in menus or dialog boxes, appear in the text like this: "Click **Build & Go**! iWebDriver will be installed on the device."

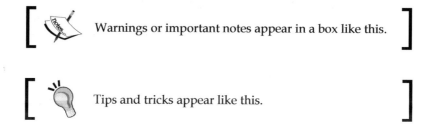

> Warnings or important notes appear in a box like this.

> Tips and tricks appear like this.

Reader feedback

Feedback from our readers is always welcome. Let us know what you think about this book—what you liked or disliked. Reader feedback is important for us as it helps us develop titles that you will really get the most out of.

To send us general feedback, simply e-mail feedback@packtpub.com, and mention the book's title in the subject of your message.

If there is a topic that you have expertise in and you are interested in either writing or contributing to a book, see our author guide at www.packtpub.com/authors.

Customer support

Now that you are the proud owner of a Packt book, we have a number of things to help you to get the most from your purchase.

Downloading the example code

You can download the example code files from your account at http://www.packtpub.com for all the Packt Publishing books you have purchased. If you purchased this book elsewhere, you can visit http://www.packtpub.com/support and register to have the files e-mailed directly to you.

Errata

Although we have taken every care to ensure the accuracy of our content, mistakes do happen. If you find a mistake in one of our books—maybe a mistake in the text or the code—we would be grateful if you could report this to us. By doing so, you can save other readers from frustration and help us improve subsequent versions of this book. If you find any errata, please report them by visiting http://www.packtpub.com/submit-errata, selecting your book, clicking on the **Errata Submission Form** link, and entering the details of your errata. Once your errata are verified, your submission will be accepted and the errata will be uploaded to our website or added to any list of existing errata under the Errata section of that title.

To view the previously submitted errata, go to https://www.packtpub.com/books/content/support and enter the name of the book in the search field. The required information will appear under the **Errata** section.

Piracy

Piracy of copyrighted material on the Internet is an ongoing problem across all media. At Packt, we take the protection of our copyright and licenses very seriously. If you come across any illegal copies of our works in any form on the Internet, please provide us with the location address or website name immediately so that we can pursue a remedy.

Please contact us at copyright@packtpub.com with a link to the suspected pirated material.

We appreciate your help in protecting our authors and our ability to bring you valuable content.

Questions

If you have a problem with any aspect of this book, you can contact us at questions@packtpub.com, and we will do our best to address the problem.

1
Getting Started with Selenium IDE

Test automation has grown in popularity over the years because developers do not have the time or money to invest in large test teams to make sure that applications work as they are expected. Developers also want to make sure that the code they have created works as they expect it to.

Jason Huggins saw this issue too and wanted to make sure that any system he was working on would work on multiple operating systems and browsers. So he created Selenium.

Selenium IDE is a fully-featured **IDE (Integrated Development Environment)** that installs as a plugin in Mozilla Firefox and enables developers to test their web applications through Selenium. With the Selenium IDE, you can record user interactions with the web browser and play them back to test for errors. It's a powerful, robust IDE that radically simplifies and automates the QA testing process.

Selenium is one of the most well-known testing frameworks in the world that is in use. It is an open source project that allows testers and developers alike to develop functional tests to drive the browser. It can be used to record workflows so that it reduces the time in regression testing. Selenium can work on any browser that supports JavaScript, since Selenium has been built using JavaScript.

In this chapter, you will learn the basics of the Selenium IDE, how to use it, and how to locate a web element on a web page. We shall cover the following topics:

- What is Selenium IDE
- Recording our first test
- Updating tests to work with AJAX sites

- Using variables in our tests
- Debugging tests
- Saving tests to be used later
- Creating and saving test suites

So, let's get on with it...

Before we start working through this chapter, we need to make sure that Mozilla Firefox is installed on your machine. If you do not have Mozilla Firefox installed, you will need to download it from `http://www.getfirefox.com/`.

Understanding Selenium IDE

Selenium IDE is a Firefox add-on developed originally by Shinya Kasatani as a way to use the original Selenium Core code without having to copy Selenium Core onto the server. **Selenium Core** is the key JavaScript module that allows Selenium to drive the browser. It has been developed using JavaScript so that it can interact with **DOM (Document Object Model)** using native JavaScript calls.

Selenium IDE was developed to allow testers and developers to record their actions as they follow the workflow that they need to test.

Installing Selenium IDE

Now that we understand what Selenium IDE is, it is a good time to install it. At the end of these steps, you will have successfully installed Selenium IDE onto your computer:

1. Go to `http://seleniumhq.org/download/`.

2. Click on the download link for Selenium IDE. You may see a message appear saying **Firefox prevented this site (seleniumhq.org) from asking you to install software on your computer**. If you do, click the **Allow** button.

3. A Firefox prompt will appear, as shown in the following screenshot:

4. You will then be asked if you would like to install Selenium IDE and the exporter add-ons. These have been made pluggable to the IDE by the work that Adam Goucher did. You will see a screenshot similar to the following one:

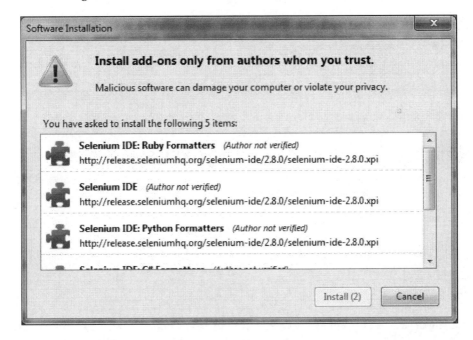

5. Click on **Install** button. This will now install Selenium IDE and formatters as Firefox add-ons.

6. Once the installation process is complete, it will ask you to restart Firefox. Click the **Restart Now** button. Firefox will close and then reopen. If you have anything open in another browser, it might be worth saving your work as Firefox will try to go back to its original state. However, this cannot be guaranteed.

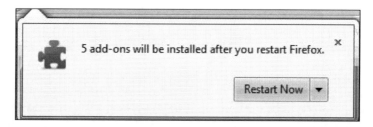

7. Once the installation is complete, the add-ons window will show the Selenium IDE and its current version:

You have successfully installed Selenium IDE and we can start thinking about writing our first test.

Getting acquainted with the Selenium IDE tool

Now that Selenium IDE has been installed, let's take some time to familiarize ourselves with it. This will give us the foundation that we can use in later chapters. Open up Selenium IDE by going through the tools menu in Mozilla Firefox. Navigate to **Tools | Selenium IDE**. A window will appear. If the menu bar is not available, which is now the default in Firefox, you can launch Selenium IDE via **Firefox | Web Developer | Selenium IDE**.

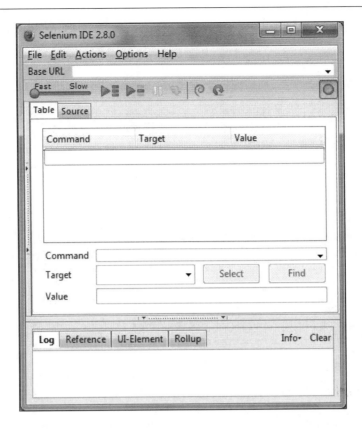

Starting from the top, I will explain what each of the items are:

- **Base URL**: This is the URL that the test will start at. All open commands will be relative to **Base URL** unless a full path is inserted in the open command.
- **Speed Slider**: This is the slider under the **Fast** and **Slow** labels in the screenshot.
- : This **play entire test suite** icon runs all the tests in the IDE.
- : This **play current test case** icon runs a single test in the IDE.
- : This **pause/resume** icon pauses a test that is currently running.
- : This **step** icon steps through the test once it has paused.
- : This is the **record** button. This will be engaged when the test is recording.

- The **Command** drop-down list has a list of all the commands that are needed to create a test. You can type into it to use the autocomplete functionality or use it as a dropdown.

- The **Target** textbox allows you to input the location of the element that you want to work against.

- The **Find** button, once the target box is populated, can be clicked to highlight the element on the page.

- The **Value** textbox is where you place the value that needs to change. For example, if you want your test to type in an input box on the web page, you will put what you want it to type in the value box.

- The **Table** tab will keep track of all your commands, targets, and values. It has been structured this way because the original version of Selenium was styled on FIT tests. **FIT (Framework for Integrated Testing)** was created by Ward Cunningham. The tests were originally designed to be run from HTML files and the IDE keeps this idea for its tests.

- If you click the **Source** tab, you will be able to see the HTML that will store the test. Each of the rows will look like this:

```
<tr>
  <td>open</td>
  <td>/chapter1</td>
  <td></td>
</tr>
```

- The area below the **Value** textbox will show the Selenium log while the tests are running. If an item fails, then it will have an [error] entry. This area will also show help on Selenium commands when you are working in the **Command** drop-down list. This can be extremely useful when typing commands into Selenium IDE instead of using the record feature.

- The **Log** tab will show a log of what is happening during the test. The **Reference** tab gives you documentation on the command that you have highlighted, and is also useful if you forgot some command; users can just start writing command in the **Command** field, then select **some like searched** and read the reference.

Rules in creating tests with Selenium IDE

Now that we have installed Selenium IDE and understand what it is, we can think about working through our first tests. There are a few things that you need to consider when creating your first test. These rules apply to any form of test automation but need to be adhered to, especially when creating tests against a user interface:

- Tests should always have a known starting point. In the context of Selenium, this can mean opening a certain page to start a workflow.

- Tests should not have to rely on any other tests to run. If a test is going to add something, do not have a separate test to delete it. This is to ensure that if something goes wrong in one test, it will not mean you have a lot of unnecessary failures to check.

- Tests should only test one thing at a time.

- Tests should clean up after themselves.

These rules, like most rules, can be broken. However, breaking them can mean that you may run into issues later on, and when you have hundreds, or even thousands of tests, these small issues can mean that large parts of a test suite are failing.

With these rules in mind, let's create our first Selenium IDE test.

Recording your first test with Selenium IDE

We will record our first test using Selenium IDE. To start recording the tests, we will need to start Mozilla Firefox. Once it has been loaded, you will need to start Selenium IDE. You will find it under the **Tools** drop-down menu in Mozilla Firefox or in the Web Developer drop-down menu. Once loaded, it will look like the next screenshot. Note that the record button is engaged when you first load the IDE.

To start recording your tests, let's do the following:

1. When in the record mode, navigate to `http://book.theautomatedtester.co.uk/chapter1`.

2. On the web application, do the following:
   1. Click on the record button (red-colored radio button).
   2. Select another value from the drop-down box, for example, **Selenium RC**.

3.   Click on the **Home Page** link.

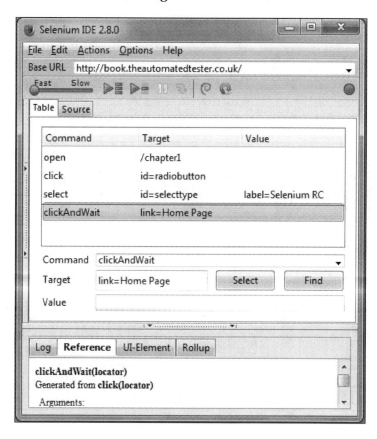

3.   Your test has now been recorded and should look like the preceding screenshot.

4.   Click the play button that looks like this icon: ▶▦

5.   Once your test has completed, it will look like the following screenshot:

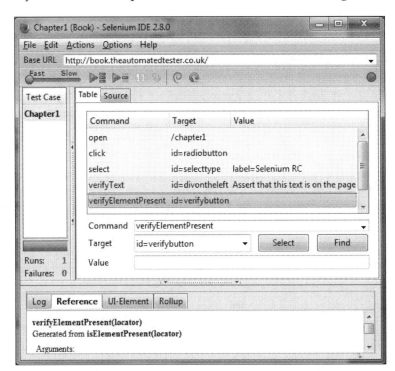

We have successfully recorded our first test and played it back. As we can see, Selenium IDE tried to apply the first rule of test automation by specifying the open command. It set the starting point of the test, in this case, **/chapter1**, and then it began stepping through the workflow that we want to record.

Once the actions have all been completed, you will see that all of the actions have a green background. This shows that they have completed successfully. On the left, you will see that it has completed one successful test, or run, within Selenium IDE. If you were to write a test that failed, the **Failure** label will have a **1** next to it.

Validating a test with assert and verify

In the last few steps, we were able to record a workflow that we would expect the user to perform. It will test that the relevant bit of functionality is there, such as buttons and links to work against. Unfortunately, we are not checking whether the other items on the page are there or if they are visible when they should be hidden. We will now work against the same page as before, but we shall make sure that different items are on the page.

There are two mechanisms for validating elements available on the application under test. The first is **assert**: this allows the test to check whether the element is on the page. If it is not available, then the test will stop on the step that failed. The second is **verify**: this allows the test to check if the element is on the page, but if it isn't, then the test will carry on execution. To add the assert or verify commands to the tests, we need to use the context menu that Selenium IDE adds to Firefox. All that one needs to do is right-click on the element if on Windows or Linux. If you have a Mac, then you will need to do the two-finger click to show the context menu.

When the context menu appears, it will look roughly like the following screenshot with the normal Firefox functions above it:

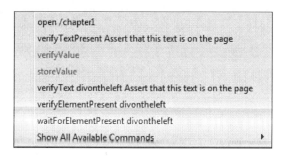

We will record the test and learn how to use/verify some commands as follows:

1. Open the IDE so that we can start recording.

2. Navigate to `http://book.theautomatedtester.co.uk/chapter1`.

3. Select **Selenium Grid** from the drop-down box.

4. Change the selection to **Selenium Grid**.

5. Verify that the **Assert that this text is on the page** text is mentioned on the right-hand side of the drop-down box, by right-clicking on the text and selecting **verifyText id=diveontheleft Assert that this text is on the page**. You can see the command in the previous screenshot.

6. Verify that the button is on the page. You will need to add a new command for `verifyElementPresent` with the `verifybutton` target in Selenium IDE.

7. Now that you have completed the previous steps, your Selenium IDE should look like the following screenshot:

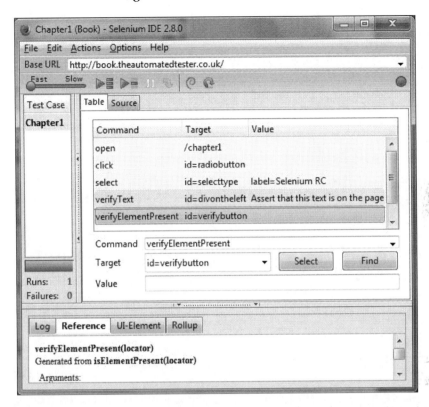

If you now run the test, you will see it has verified that what you are expecting to see on the page has appeared. Notice that the verify commands have a darker green color. This is to show that they are more important to the test than moving through the steps. The test has now checked that the text we required is on the page and that the button is there too.

What will happen if the verify command did not find what it was expecting? The IDE would have thrown an error stating what was expected was not there, but then carried on with the rest of the test. We can see an example of this in the following screenshot:

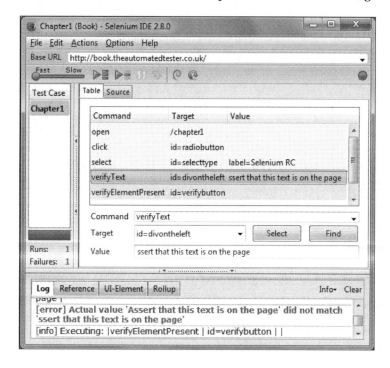

The test would not have carried on if it was using assert as the mechanism for validating that the elements and text were loaded with the page.

We have just seen that we can add asserts or verification to the page. Selenium IDE does not do this when recording, so it will always be a manual step. The assert command will stop the running tests, unlike the verify command in which the tests will continue running even after failure. In both the cases, Selenium IDE will log an error. Each of these have their own merits.

Some of the verify and assert methods are as follows:

Selenium Command	Command Description
verifyElementPresent	This verifies an expected element is present on the page.
assertElementPresent	This asserts an expected element is present on the page.
verifyElementNotPresent	This verifies an expected element is not present on the page.

Selenium Command	Command Description
assertElementNotPresent	This asserts an expected element is not present on the page.
verifyText	This verifies expected text and its corresponding HTML tags are present on the page.
assertText	This asserts expected text and its corresponding HTML tags are present on the page.
verifyAttribute	This verifies the value of an attribute of any HTML tag on the page.
assertAttribute	This asserts the value of an attribute of any HTML tag on the page.
verifyChecked	This verifies whether the condition of the checkbox is checked or not on the page.
assertChecked	This asserts whether the condition of the checkbox is checked or not on the page.
verifyAlert	This verifies the alert present on the page.
assertAlert	This asserts the alert present on the page.
verifyTitle	This verifies an expected page title.
assertTitle	This asserts an expected page title.

Creating comments in your tests

Before we carry on further with Selenium, this is a good time to mention how to create comments in your tests. As all good software developers know, having readable code and having comments can make maintenance in the future much easier. Unlike in software development, it is extremely hard, almost impossible, to write self-documenting code. To combat this, it is good practice to make sure that your tests have comments that future software testers can use.

Adding Selenium IDE comments

To add comments to your tests, perform the following steps:

1. In the test that was created earlier, right-click on a step. For example, the verify step.

2. The Selenium IDE context menu will be visible as shown in the following screenshot:

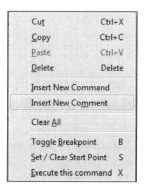

3. Click on **Insert New Comment**. A space will appear between the Selenium commands.

4. Click on the **Command** textbox and enter in a comment so that you can use it for future maintenance. It will look like the following screenshot:

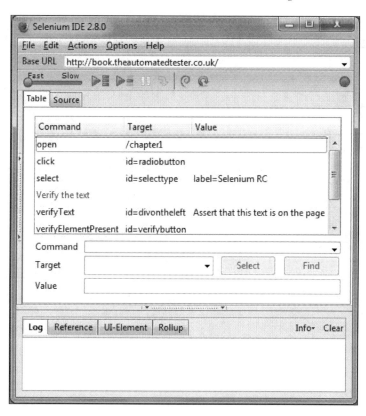

We just had a look at how to create comments. Comments will always appear as purple text in the IDE. This, like in most IDEs, is to help you spot comments quicker when looking through your test cases. Now that we know how to keep our tests maintainable with comments, let's carry on working with Selenium IDE to record/tweak/replay our scripts.

Multiplying windows

Web applications, unfortunately, do not live in one window of your browser. An example of this can be a site that shows reports. Most reports will have their own window so that people can easily move between them.

Unfortunately, in testing terms, this can be quite difficult to do, but in this section, we will have a look at creating a test that can move between windows.

Working with multiple windows

Working with multiple browser windows can be one of the most difficult things to do within a Selenium test. This is down to the fact that the browser needs to allow Selenium to programmatically know how many child browser processes have been spawned.

In the following examples, we will see the tests click on an element on the page that will cause a new window to appear. If you have a pop-up blocker running, it's a good idea to disable it for this site while you work through these examples. Open up Selenium IDE and go to the **Chapter 1** page on the site and refer to the following steps:

1. Click on one of the elements on the page that has the text **Click this link to launch another window**. This will cause a small window to appear.

2. Verify the text in the popup by right-clicking and selecting **VerifyText id=popup text within the popup window**.

3. Once the window has loaded, click on the **Close the Window** text inside it.

4. Add a verify command for an element on the page. Your test should now look like the following screenshot:

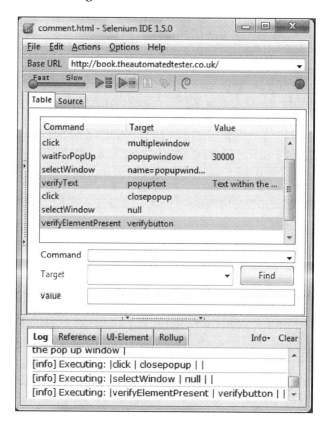

Sometimes, Selenium IDE will add a `clickAndWait` command instead of a `click` command. This is because it notices that the page has to unload. If this happens, just change the `clickAndWait` command to a `click` so that it does not cause a timeout in the test.

In the test script, we can see that it has clicked on the item to load the new window and then has inserted a `waitForPopUp` command. This is so that your test knows that it has to wait for a web server to handle the request and the browser to render the page. Any commands that require a page to load from a web server will have a `waitFor` command. The next command is the `selectWindow` command. This command tells Selenium IDE that it will need to switch context to the window, called `popupwindow`, and will execute all the commands that follow in that window unless told otherwise by a later command.

Once the test has finished with the pop-up window, it will need to return to the parent window from where it started. To do this, we need to specify `null` as the window. This will force the `selectWindow` command to move the context of the test back to its parent window.

Complex working with multiple windows

In this example, we will open two pop-up windows and move between them and the parent window as it completes its steps:

1. Start Selenium IDE and go to **Chapter 1** on the website.

2. Click on the **Click this link to launch another window** link. This will launch a pop-up window.

3. Assert the text on the page. We do this by right-clicking and selecting **assertText**.

4. Go back to the parent window and click on the link to launch the second pop-up window.

5. Verify the text on the page.

6. Move to the first pop-up window and close it using the close link. As before, be aware of `clickAndWait` instead of click.

7. Move to the second pop-up window and close it using the close link.

8. Move back to the parent window and verify an element on that page.

9. Run your test and watch how it moves between the windows. When complete, it should look like the following screenshot:

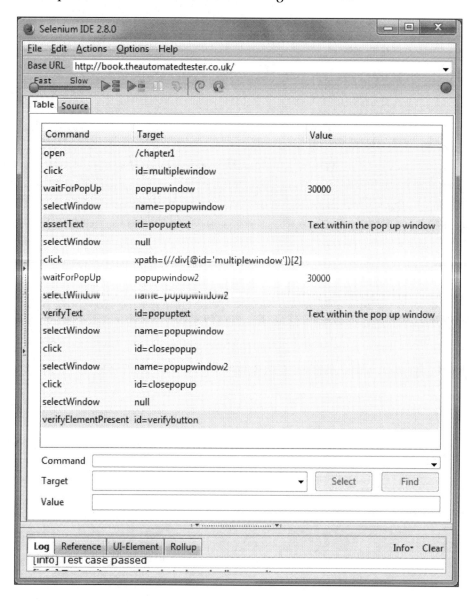

We just had a look at creating a test that can move between multiple windows. We saw how we can move between the child windows and its parent window as though we were a user.

Selenium tests against AJAX applications

Web applications today are being designed in such a way that they appear the same as desktop applications. Web developers are accomplishing this by using AJAX within their web applications. **AJAX (Asynchronous JavaScript And XML)** relies on JavaScript creating asynchronous calls and then returning XML with the data that the user or application requires to carry on. AJAX does not rely on XML anymore, as more and more people move over to **JSON (JavaScript Object Notation)**, which is more lightweight in the way it transfers the data. It does not rely on the extra overhead of opening and closing tags that is needed to create valid XML.

Working on pages with AJAX

In our example, we will click on a link and then assert that some text is visible on the screen:

1. Start up Selenium IDE and make sure that the record button is pressed.

2. Navigate to `http://book.theautomatedtester.co.uk/chapter1`.

3. Click on the text that says **Click this link to load a page with AJAX**.

4. Verify the text that appears on your screen. Your test should look like the following screenshot:

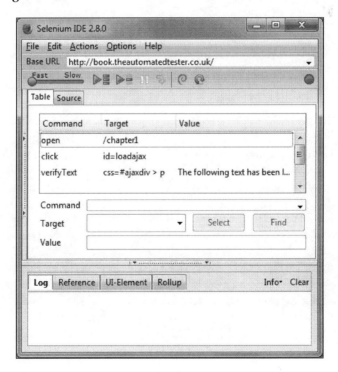

5. Run the test that you have created. When it has finished running, it should look like the following screenshot:

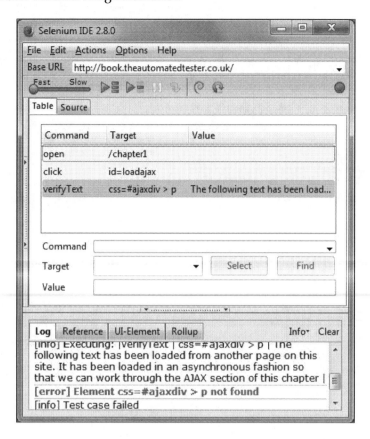

Have a look at the page that you are working against. Can you see the text that the test is expecting? You should see it, so why has this test failed? The test has failed because when the test reached that point, the element containing the text was not loaded into the DOM. This is because it was being requested and rendered from the web server into the browser.

To remedy this issue, we will need to add a new command to our test so that our tests pass in the future:

1. Right-click on the step that failed so that the Selenium IDE context menu appears.
2. Click on **Insert New Command**.

3. In the **Command** select box, type `waitForElementPresent` or select it from the drop-down menu.

4. In the **Target** box, add the target that is used in the `verifyText` command.

5. Run the test again and it should pass this time:

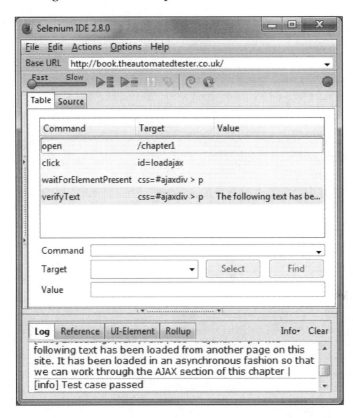

Selenium does not implicitly wait for the item that it needs to interact with, so it is seen as good practice to wait for the item you need to work with and then interact with it. The `waitFor` commands will timeout after 30 seconds by default, but if you need it to wait longer, you can specify the tests by using the `setTimeout` command. This will set the timeout value that the tests will use in future commands.

If need be, you can change the default wait if you go to **Options | Options** and then on the **General** tab, and under **Default timeout value of recorded command in milliseconds** (*30s = 30,000ms*) change it to what you want. Remember, *1,000 milliseconds = 1 second*.

Working with AJAX applications

As more and more applications try to act like desktop applications, we need to be able to handle synchronization steps between our test and our application. In this section, we will see how to handle AJAX and what to synchronize:

1. Navigate to `http://book.theautomatedtester.co.uk/chapter1`.

2. Click on the **load text to the page** button.

3. Wait for the text **I have been added with a timeout**. Your test will look like the following screenshot:

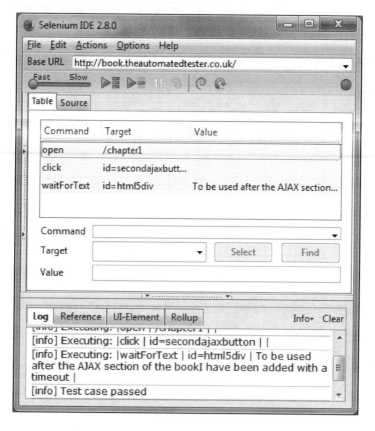

In the previous examples, we waited for an element to appear on the page; there are a number of different commands that we can use to wait. Also, remember that we can take advantage of waiting for something not to be on the page, for example, `waitForElementNotPresent`. This can be just as effective as waiting for it to be there.

The following commands make up the `waitFor` set of commands, but this is not an exhaustive list:

Selenium Command	Command Description
waitForAlertNotPresent	This waits for an alert to disappear from the page.
waitForAlertPresent	This waits for an alert to appear on the page.
waitForElementPresent	This waits for an expected element to appear on the page.
waitForElementNotPresent	This waits for an expected element to disappear from the page.
waitForTextPresent	This waits for expected text and its corresponding HTML tags to appear on the page.
waitForTextNotPresent	This waits for expected text and its corresponding HTML tags to disappear from the page.
waitForPageToLoad	This waits for all elements to appear on the expected page.
waitForFrameToLoad	This waits for an expected frame and its corresponding HTML tags to appear on the page.

A number of these commands are run implicitly when other commands are being run. An example of this is the `clickAndWait` command. This will fire off a `click` command and then fire off a `waitForPageToLoad` command. Another example is the `open` command, which only completes when the page has fully loaded.

If you are feeling confident, then it's a good time to try different `waitFor` command techniques.

Storing information from the page in the test

Sometimes, there is a need to store elements that are on the page to be used later in a test. It could be that your test needs to pick a date that is on the page and use it later so that you do not need to hardcode values into your test.

Once the element has been stored, you will be able to use it again by requesting it from a JavaScript dictionary that Selenium keeps track of. To use the variable, it will take one of the following two formats: it can look like `${variableName}` or `storedVars['variableName']`. I prefer the `storedVars` format as it follows the same format as within Selenium internals. To see how this works, let's work through the following example:

1. Open up Selenium IDE and switch off the record button.

2. Navigate to `http://book.theautomatedtester.co.uk/chapter1`.

3. Right-click on the text **Assert that this text is on the page** and go to the `storeText` command in the context menu and click on it.

4. A dialog will appear as shown in the following screenshot. Enter the name of a variable that you want to use. I have used `textOnThePage` as the name of my variable.

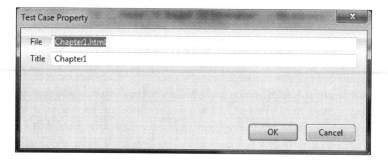

5. Click on the row below the `storeText` command in Selenium IDE.

6. Type `type` into the **Command** textbox.

7. Type `storeinput` into the **Target** box.

8. Type `${textOnThePage}` into the **Value** box.

9. Run the test. It should look like the following screenshot:

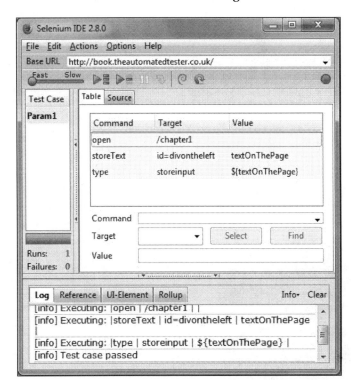

Once your test has completed running, you will see that it has placed **Assert that this text is on the page** into the textbox.

Debugging tests

We have successfully created a number of tests and have seen how we can work against AJAX applications, but unfortunately, creating tests that run perfectly the first time can be difficult. Sometimes, as a test automator, you will need to debug your tests to see what is wrong.

To work through this part of the chapter, you will need to have a test open in Selenium IDE.

These two steps are quite useful when your tests are not running and you want to execute a specific command. They are:

1. Highlight a command.

2. Press the X key. This will make the command execute in Selenium IDE.

When a test is running, you can press the pause button to pause the test after the step that is currently being run. Once the test has been paused, the step button is no longer disabled and you can press it to step through the test as if you were stepping through an application.

If you are having issues with elements on the page, you can type in their location and then click on the **Find** button. This will surround the element that you are looking for with a green border that flashes for a few seconds. It should look like the following screenshot:

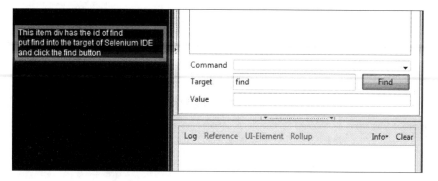

The echo command is also a good way to write something from your test to the log. This is equivalent to the `Console.log` code in JavaScript, for example, `echo | ${textOnThePage}`, as shown in the following screenshot:

Also, remember that if you are trying to debug a test script that you have created with Selenium IDE, you can set breakpoints in your test. You simply right-click on the line and select breakpoint from the list. It will be similar to the following screenshot:

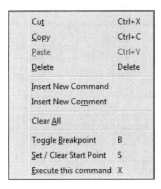

You can also use the keyboard shortcut of **B** to allow you to do it quicker.

Creating test suites

We managed to create a number of tests using Selenium IDE and have managed to run them successfully. The next thing to have a look at is how to create a test suite, so that we can open the test suite and then have it run a number of tests that we have created. If you have Selenium IDE open from the last steps, click on the **File** menu:

1. Click **New Test Case**.

2. You will see that Selenium IDE has opened a new area on the left of the IDE as shown in the following screenshot:

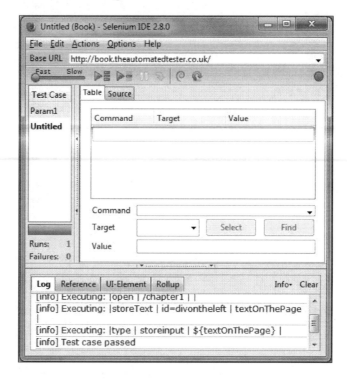

You can do this as many times as you want, and when the **Play entire test suite** button is clicked, it will run all the tests in the test suite. It will log all the passes and failures at the bottom of the **Test Case** box.

To save this, click on the **File** menu and then click **Save Test Suite** and save the test suite file to a place where you can get to it again. One thing to note is that saving a test suite does not save the test case. Make sure that you save the test case every time you make a change and not just the test suite.

To change the name of the test case to something a lot more meaningful, you can do this by right-clicking on the test and clicking on the **Properties** item in the context menu:

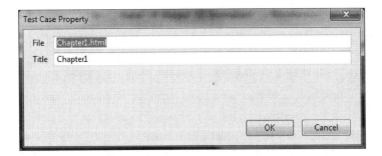

You can now add meaningful names to your tests and they will appear in Selenium IDE instead of falling back to their filenames.

We have managed to create our first test suite. This can be used to group tests together to be used later. If your tests have been saved, you can update the test suite properties to give the tests a name that is easier to read.

Parameterization

Parameterization is a key feature in automation testing. It is possible to give test data (parameter) as input in Selenium IDE as it is with any other automation tool. Selenium IDE requires configuration before proceeding for parameterization, which is explained in the following section.

After configuring Selenium IDE for parameterization, in the following example, we will search a text on Google and verify the text appears on the page. The storeEval command will read the search data from the google_search.js file and save it in the searchDataValue variable. With this variable, data types on the Google search page, verify **Download Selenium IDE** text using the assertTextPresent command. In this way, you can achieve data parameterization or data-driven testing by passing external data to a variable in Selenium IDE.

Selenium IDE Configuration

You need to create JavaScript file as the data source file. These are the steps to create JavaScript file and configure Selenium IDE:

1. In a Notepad, create input data as follows:

    ```
    searchData = 'Selenium IDE'
    ```

2. Save it as a file, say for example, `google_search.js`.

3. Open Selenium IDE and choose the **Option | Options...** menu.

4. Under Selenium IDE Extensions, browse the saved `google_search.js` file. After attaching the data file, your Selenium IDE option window will look like the following screenshot. Then, click **OK** and restart the Selenium IDE:

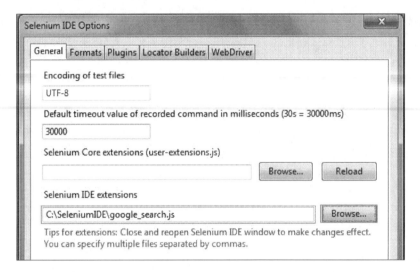

5. Now, record the script to perform Google search and verify the page element and update the commands as shown in the following screenshot. Then, execute the test. You can also use the `WaitForElementPresent` command till the page element is loaded and verify instead of the `pause` command.

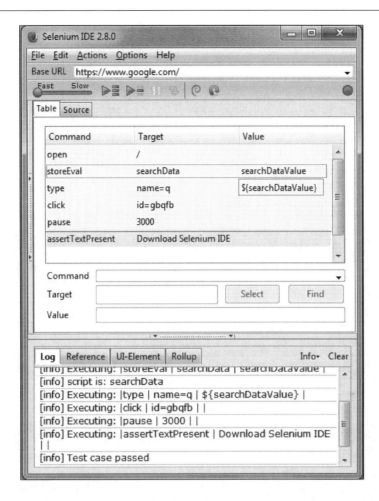

In this example, we are searching a text on the Google page and verifying the text appearing on the page. The `storeEval` command will read the search data from the `google_search.js` file and store it in a `searchDataValue` variable and verify the **Download Selenium IDE** text using an `assertTextPresent` command. In this way, you can achieve data parameterization or data-driven testing in Selenium IDE.

Generating source code from Selenium IDE

The Selenium IDE formatters plugin enables you to export the recorded steps. Selenium IDE can export the recorded steps or user actions to different formats. The Selenium team provides bindings for several programming languages. You can write a script in one of these programming languages and use the provided libraries to remotely control a browser. Selenium IDE formatters convert the recorded actions into source code for a specific programming language.

You need to set enable experimental features on Selenium IDE options to view the formatters. Check out the following screenshot for formatters:

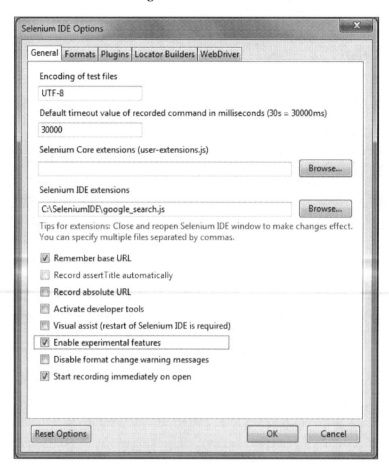

Record user actions on Selenium IDE, and to view specific programming language formatters, select the **Selenium IDE | Options | Format** as shown in the following screenshot. A confirmation dialog appears, click on **OK**:

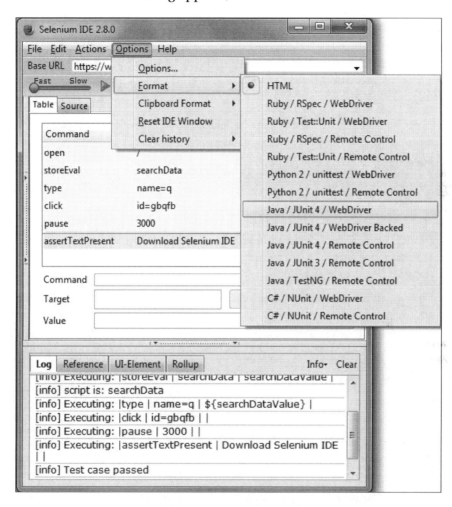

Ensure that the code is displayed under the Selenium IDE **Source** tab as seen in the screenshot that follows. You can also see the **Java/Junit4/WebDriver** programming language formatter. Selenium IDE used the type command to identify text typing into the textbox. In the source code, the sendkeys command is used in order to type text into the textbox using the Selenium Java/Junit4/WebDriver programming language. You can generate a formatter of any of the specific programming languages. After viewing the source code, you can switch back from a specific formatter to HTML. If a formatter is not HTML, then recording options will not work and the **Table** tab will not be active:

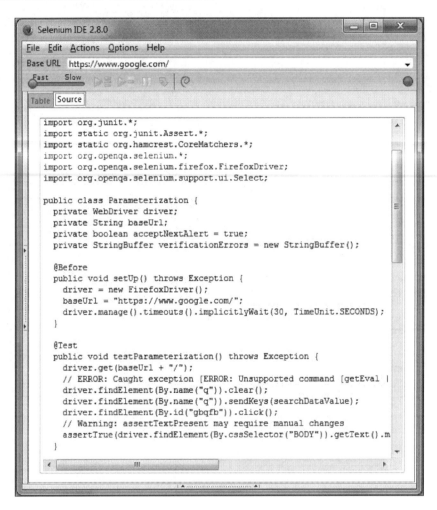

In the preceding recorded action, we searched a text on Google and verified the text appears on the page. Selenium IDE exports these actions to view a specific programming language. This is one of the useful features of Selenium IDE; it provides an option to set the clipboard format. You can copy commands from the **Table** tab and paste in the format of that specific programming language.

Saving tests

Saving tests is done in the same manner as saving a test suite. Click on the **File** menu and then click **Save Test Case**. This will give you a **Save** dialog box; save this to a place where you can get to it later. When you save your tests and your test suite, Selenium IDE will try to keep the relationships between the folders in step when saving the tests and the test suites.

What you cannot record

We have seen our tests work really well by recording them and then playing them back. Unfortunately, there are a number of things that Selenium cannot do. Since Selenium was developed in JavaScript, it tries to synthesize what the user does with JavaScript events. This means that it is bound by the same rules that JavaScript has in any browsers by operating within the sandbox.

- Silverlight and Flex/Flash applications, at the time of writing, cannot be recorded with Selenium IDE. Both these technologies operate in their own sandbox and do not operate with the DOM to do their work. HTML5, at the time of writing, is not fully supported with Selenium IDE. A good example of this is elements that have the contentEditable=true attribute. If you want to see this, you can use the type command to type something into the html5div element. The test will tell you that it has completed the command, but the UI will not have changed, as shown in the following screenshot:

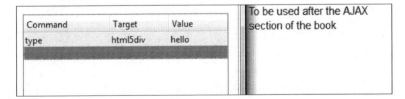

- Selenium IDE does not work with Canvas elements on the page either, so you will not be able to make your tests move items around on a page.

- Selenium cannot do file uploads. This is due to the JavaScript sandbox not allowing JavaScript to interact with `<input type=file>` elements on a page. While you might be able to send the text to the box, it will not always do what you expect, so I would recommend not doing it.

We will be able to automate a number of these elements with **Selenium WebDriver** in later chapters of this book.

Summary

We learned a lot in this chapter about Selenium IDE, learning how to create your first test using the record and replay functions and we now understand some of the basic concepts such as moving between multiple windows that can appear in a test, and saving our tests for future use.

Specifically, we covered the following topics:

- **How to install Selenium IDE**: We started by downloading Selenium IDE from `http://seleniumhq.org`.

- **What Selenium IDE is made up of**: The breakup of Selenium IDE allowed us to see what makes up Selenium IDE. It allowed us to understand the different parts that make up a command that will be executed in a test as well as its basic format. We had a look at how to load Selenium IDE and how to get started with recording tests. We saw that a Selenium IDE command is made up of three sections: the command, the target, and the value that might be used.

- **Recording and replaying tests**: We used Selenium IDE to record a workflow that a user will need in their tests. We also had a look at verifying and asserting that elements are on the page and that the text we are expecting is also on the page.

- **How to add comments to tests**: In this section of the chapter, we saw how to add comments to the tests so that they are more maintainable.

- **Working with multiple windows**: In this section, we saw how applications today can have pop-up windows that tests need to be able to move between.

- **Working with AJAX applications**: AJAX applications do not have the items needed for the tests when the tests get to commands. To get around this, we had a look at adding `waitFor` commands to the tests. This is due to the fact that Selenium does not implicitly wait for elements to appear on the page.

- **Storing information in variables**: There is always something that is on the page that needs to be used later, but unfortunately, you will not know what the value is before the test runs. This section showed us how we can record items into a variable and use it later in a test. This can be something that has happened on a page and needs to be checked that it is still there on later pages.

- **Debugging tests**: Creating tests does not always go according to the plan, so in this section, we saw some of the different ways to debug your tests.

- **Parameterization**: Parameterizing the data in Selenium IDE.

- **Saving test suites**: Finally, we saw how we can save tests for future use and how we can save them into different groups by saving them into test suites.

We also discussed what cannot be tested using Selenium IDE. We saw that Silverlight and Flex/Flash applications cannot be tested, and that when working with a number of HTML5 elements, the tests say that they have completed the tasks even though the UI has not changed. In later chapters, we will discuss different mechanisms that we can use within our tests that might be useful against HTML5 elements on the page.

Now that we've learnt about Selenium IDE, we're ready to look at all the different techniques we can use to find elements on the page.

Self-test questions

1. What is the main language that drives Selenium IDE?

    1. Ruby.

    2. Python.

    3. JavaScript.

2. Selenium IDE works on Internet Explorer.

    1. True.

    2. False.

3. Selenium verifies items on the page when it is recording steps.

   1. True.
   2. False.

4. What is the difference between verify and assert?

5. If you wanted to validate that a button had appeared on a page, which two commands would be the best to use?

   1. verifyTextPresent / assertTextPresent.
   2. verifyElementPresent / assertElementPresent.
   3. verifyAlertPresent / assertAlertPresent.
   4. verifyAlert / assertAlert.

6. If an element got added after the page loaded, what command would you use to make sure the test passed in the future?

   1. waitForElementPresent.
   2. pause.
   3. assertElementPresent.

7. How do we run all the tests in a test suite?

2
Locators

Locators allow us to find elements on a page that can be used in our tests. In the last chapter, we managed to work against a page that had decent locators. In HTML, it is seen as a good practice to make sure that every element you need to interact with has an ID attribute and a name attribute. Unfortunately, following best practices can be extremely difficult, especially when building HTML dynamically on the server before sending it back to the browser.

In this chapter, we will cover the following topics:

- Locate elements by ID
- Locate elements by name
- Locate elements by link
- Locate elements by XPath
- Locate elements by CSS
- Locate elements by DOM

So, let's get on with it.

 Before starting this chapter, we should begin by making sure that we have all the relevant applications installed. While these are not foolproof, they will give us an idea of how to construct the locator for our tests.

The following are the browser add-ons that will help us inspect and locate the web elements:

- **Firebug**: Firebug (`https://addons.mozilla.org/firefox/addon/firebug`) has become the de facto tool for web developers as it allows them to find elements on the page by using the find functionality. It has a JavaScript **REPL** (**Read-Eval-Print-Loop**) or an interactive shell that allows you to run JavaScript without having to create an entire page.

- **Firefinder**: Firefinder (`https://addons.mozilla.org/firefox/addon/firefinder-for-firebug`) is a very good tool for testing out XPath and CSS on the page. It will highlight all elements on the page that match the selector to your element location.

- **IE Developer Tools**: This is a built-in tool in IE7, IE8, and IE9 that we can launch by pressing *F12*. It also has a number of features that Firebug has in common with.

- **Google Chrome Developer Tools**: This, like IE, is a built-in feature in the browser and will also allow you to find elements on the page and be able to work out its XPath.

Once you have worked out your locator, you will need to put it into Selenium IDE to test it, and verify that the element is located properly. In the layout of Selenium IDE, one of the buttons on the page is named **Find**. Click on this button when you have something in the **Value** textbox; it will highlight the item in green, as shown in the following screenshot. On Mac OS X, the background color will flash yellow:

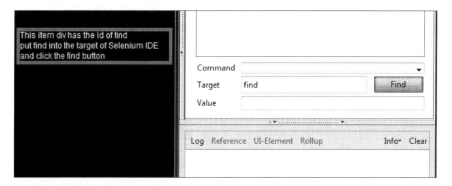

Now that we have these tools and understand how to use them, we can start adding locators to our test scripts.

Locating elements by ID

On web applications today, elements should have an ID attribute for all their controls on the page. A control is an element that we can interact with and is not static text. This allows Selenium to find the unique item, since IDs are unique, and then complete the action that it needs to do against that element. ID locators usually have the highest speed, especially when compared to XPath.

Finding IDs of elements on the page with Firebug

In this section, we will find a web button with an ID that is on the page. You will need to have Firebug installed for this. We will look at how to find the ID of an element using Firefox:

1. Navigate to `http://book.theautomatedtester.co.uk/chapter2` and click on the Firebug icon present in the Firefox browser toolbar shown in the following screenshot, or start Firebug by pressing the *F12* key:

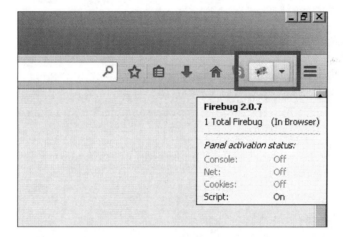

2. Click on the **Select Element** icon in Firebug.
3. Move your mouse over the element that you wish to have a look at.

4. Move your mouse over different elements. As you can see in the following screenshot, Firebug will highlight each of the items that you want to see:

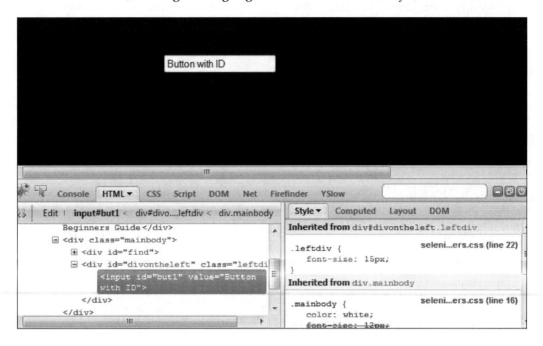

Once a web page element has been selected, you can see that the element and all of the different attributes are now visible. We saw that the item got highlighted, or a single color box surrounded it, so that we can see which item is selected. We can see this in the previous screenshot.

Now that we are confident on how to find elements and their attributes, let's start using them in Selenium.

Finding elements by ID

Elements often have IDs that are used to locate them. In the **Target** textbox, this will look like id=Element. Follow this example to see how it works:

1. Open Selenium IDE.

2. Navigate to http://book.theautomatedtester.co.uk/chapter2 and click on the Firebug icon.

3. Find any element that you want to interact with on the page and, in the **Target** textbox of Selenium IDE, place its ID attribute value. Make sure that it has an ID attribute. For example, use but1 as in the preceding screenshot against http://book.theautomatedtester.co.uk/chapter2.

4. Type the `click` command into the **Command** select box.

5. Play your script.

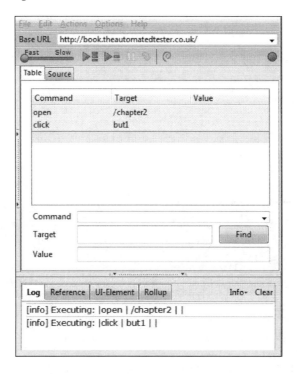

Your test will have executed the step successfully. Since the test is using the ID of the element, if that element were to be moved around, it would find the item without any issue. This is one of the main plus points of Selenium over a lot of the competing test frameworks out there.

Moving elements on the page

As I just mentioned, Selenium, when using the value of the ID attribute, can find elements on a page even if they are moved. Click on the button with the text **Random** on the **Chapter 2** page of the site (you can do this manually), and then run the script that we created earlier. You will see that your test executes successfully.

Finding elements by name

Elements do not necessarily have ID attributes on all of them. Elements can have names that we can use to locate them. In the **Target** textbox, this would look like `name=Element`. Try the following example to see how it works:

1. Open Selenium IDE.

2. Navigate to `http://book.theautomatedtester.co.uk/chapter2` and click on the Firebug icon.

3. Find any element that you want to interact with and, in the **Target** textbox of Selenium IDE, place the value of its name attribute. For example, use `but2`, as in the following screenshot, against `http://book.theautomatedtester. co.uk/chapter2`:

4. Type the `click` command into the **Command** select box.

5. Play your script.

Your test will have executed the step successfully. Since the test used the name of the element, if that element were to be moved around, it would find the item without any issue.

Adding filters to the name

There are times when there may be elements on the page that have the same name but a different attribute. When this happens, we can apply filters to the locator so that Selenium IDE can find the element that we are after. An example of this on the page is `name=verifybutton1 value=chocolate;`. This will find the second button with the name `verifybutton1`. See an example of this in the following screenshot:

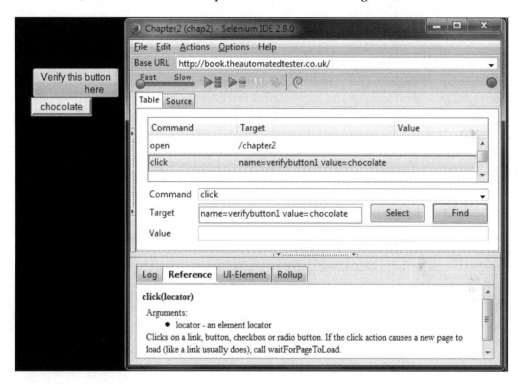

Finding elements by link text

The most common element on a page is a link. Links allow pages to be joined together so that end users can navigate a site with confidence. You can see a screenshot of the element being found in Selenium IDE:

1. To specify that you want to follow a link, you use the `link=link` target.

2. On `http://book.theautomatedtester.co.uk/chapter2`, there is a link to the `index` page of the site. In the **Target** textbox in Selenium IDE, we will need to add `link=Index`. If you click the **Find** button on Selenium IDE, you will see the following screenshot:

We have seen how we can find links that are on that page so that they can be used in your test. All that is needed is the inner text of the nodes in the DOM.

Finding elements by accessing the DOM via JavaScript

There are times when the DOM will be updated via AJAX and this means that the locator needed for the test needs some form of JavaScript to see if it is there. In JavaScript, calling the DOM to find the first link on the page looks like `document.links[0];`. The `document` element represents the HTML document and `links` is an array on that object. On the `Chapter 2` page of the website, it will show the link that we used in the previous sections of this chapter.

However, normally, it will just be calls to the DOM to see if an element has been added as in the following screenshot:

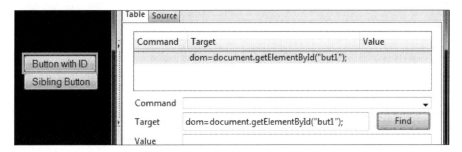

We have just seen that we can use JavaScript to find elements on a page. This can be extremely useful if you have a web application that does a lot of interaction with the DOM.

Finding elements by XPath

Unfortunately, best practices cannot always be followed when building the markup or, if they are, then they may have a dynamic edge to them. An example of this is working against a page that uses a key from the database as the element ID, so when something is edited and stored back in the database, it can be found a lot quicker and updated. In this section of the chapter, we will work with XPath. XPath allows us to query the DOM as though it were an XML document. With XPath, we can execute some rather complex queries to find elements on the page that may not have been accessible otherwise.

Let's start by creating a basic XPath. We will look for an input button:

1. Open Selenium IDE.
2. Navigate to `http://book.theautomatedtester.co.uk/chapter2`.
3. Type `click` into the **Command** select box.
4. Type `xpath=//input` into the **Target** textbox.
5. Click on the **Find** button. It will find a button on the page as in the following screenshot. Note that sometimes Selenium IDE flashes the button in a yellow color:

Your test will have looked against the DOM to find an element that was of the `input` type. The `xpath=` value at the beginning tells Selenium that the element needed will be located by XPath. It removes the guesswork that Selenium will have to do and is seen as good practice. The `//` tells the query that it needs to stop at the first element that it finds. It is a greedy query so, if you have a rather large web page, it can take some time to return since it will try to parse the page. Writing the XPath like this allows us to make changes to the UI, within reason, without it impacting the test.

Using direct XPath in your test

As I mentioned in the first part of this section, having // as the start of your XPath is seen as a greedy query since it will parse the entire DOM until it finds the element that you want to find. If you want to work against an element that is always in a certain place, you can use a more direct XPath.

Finding elements by direct XPath

Instead of using //, you can use a single /, but you will need to make sure that the first node in your query is HTML. Let's see an example of this:

1. Open Selenium IDE.
2. Navigate to `http://book.theautomatedtester.co.uk/chapter2`.
3. Type `xpath=/html/body/div[2]/div[3]/input` into the **Target** input of Selenium IDE.
4. Click on the **Find** button.

The previous locator will find the same element as before. This type of XPath query will find the element fractionally quicker, but if your UI is going to change, it may fail if the element is moved into a different area of the page. One thing to really note is that XPath locators can be extremely fragile. They can find what you want, but when you make a small change to your HTML, they will break, meaning that you need to do maintenance on that test. I would recommend using these only if you have to.

You may have noticed that parent and child nodes are in the same query. Since HTML has a tree structure, it just notifies the query that it needs to start at the HTML node, then move to its child node, body, then to the body's child, and so on until it reaches the end of the query. Once it has done this, it will stop executing the query.

Using XPath to find the nth element of a type

There are a lot of occasions when, as a Selenium user, you will have to click on an edit button in a table so that you can update something specific. Have a look at the button that you wish to click; it does not have a unique name or ID. An example of this is the button with the value *Sibling Button*.

When doing a query against the DOM, an array of elements is returned to Selenium that matches the query. For example, if you were to do //div on the Chapter 2 page of the website, there are three elements returned to Selenium. If your test only depends on the first item in your test, then it will try and access only the first item. If you want to interact with the second element, then your query will look like //div[2]. Note that the *second* to *nth* element need to be sibling nodes of the first element that is returned. If they are not and you were to access the element, it will fail, saying that it could not find them.

We can see this with the input buttons that are present on the page. They all reside in their own containing div element, so do not have any sibling elements that are also input elements. If you were to put //input[2] into Selenium IDE, it will not be able to find the element and fail.

You can see an example of this in the following screenshot:

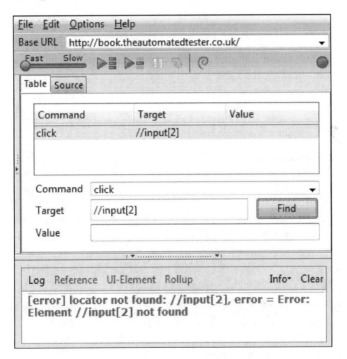

Using element attributes in XPath queries

There are times when you need to find elements that are the same except for one or two attributes. To handle this, we can add the attributes to the query so that we can try to make the element more unique for use in the test. The format can be used for any attribute on any element. It will always follow `xpath=//element[@attribute='attribute value']`. For example, if you have two `div` elements on the page, but they only differ in the class attribute, your XPath query will look like the following: `xpath=//div[@class='classname']`.

Try doing this with Selenium yourself by trying to identify something unique about the `div` elements on the page. When you have completed the task, your query should look like one of these shown in the following screenshot:

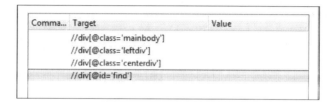

Performing partial match on attribute content

As mentioned earlier, there are times when there is no way for a developer to create a static ID for elements on the page. This can be down to the fact that the element is being loaded asynchronously via AJAX or because it is using the key of the data as it is stored in the database.

There are times where only part of the ID is dynamic. This is to allow the developer to cram more information onto the page so that the user has everything they need. We need to have a mechanism to work with these elements. To make a partial match, your query needs to have the word `contains` with the attribute and the partial match that it needs. For example, if you want to access the element with the following text in it *This element has an ID that changes every time the page is loaded*, you use `//div[contains(@id, 'time_')]`. This is due to the first part of the ID always being static. The locator can also use `starts-with` instead of `contains` to make the XPath query stricter in what is returned. The queries in the following screenshot find the same element on the page:

Table	Source	

Comma...	Target	Value
	//div[starts-with(@id,'time_')]	
	//div[contains(@id,'time_')]	

Finding an element by the text it contains

Finding elements by the text they contain can be quite useful when working with web pages that have been created dynamically. The elements can be obtained by using a web-based WYSIWYG editor, or you might just like to find a paragraph on the page with specific text to then do further queries.

To do this, your query will need to have the `text()` method called in the query. It will match the entire contents of the node if it has the `//element[text()='inner text']` format. As seen in the previous section, your query can use the `contains` keyword to a bit more leniency in what it finds. Next, you can find a screenshot of queries that find the same element as the previous section:

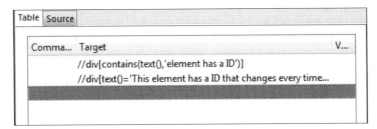

Leveraging the XPath axis with elements

As we have seen, XPath is normally only used if the element we need to interact with is not accessible by normal means. In this section of the chapter, we will have a look at leveraging the XPath axis in our queries to find the element that we wish to interact with. An example that I have used in the real world was to find a table cell that had specific text, then traverse the tree backwards to find the edit button so that I can click on it. This may seem laborious just to click on an edit button, but it is extremely common according to the Selenium users forum on Google Groups.

Using the XPath axis

In the first example, we found a button and then its sibling. In this example, the query that we will generate is equivalent to `xpath=//div[@class='leftdiv']/input[2]`.

1. We will start by finding the first element for our query, which is `//input[@value='Button with ID']`. Place this element into the Selenium IDE Target textbox and see which element it highlights.

2. There is another button below the one that is highlighted and that is the element that we need to work with in this section. The button is the next input item in the HTML, so it the element, `following-sibling`, that we need. Our locator will look like `//input[@value='Button with ID']/` `following-sibling::input[@value='Sibling Button']`, and if it was placed into Selenium IDE, it will be able to find the element that we are after; see the following screenshot:

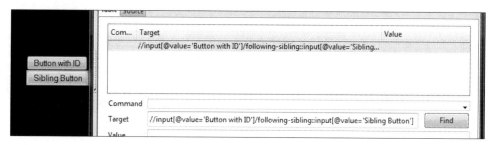

We just saw how we can use the XPath axis (an axis defines a node-set relative to the current node) to find the elements that we need in our tests. We managed to find the element using the `following-sibling` axis. As mentioned earlier, you can use XPath to find an element and then walk backwards up the tree. If we were to take the preceding example and reverse it, you would need to start at the button with the value **Sibling Button** and then go back to the button with the value **Button with ID** the XPath query would then look like. Finding the element using the Xpath axis is shown in the following screenshot:

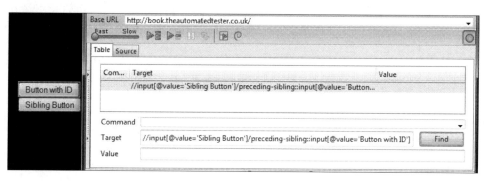

The following is a list of axes that you can use in your XPath queries to find the elements on the page:

Axis name	Result
ancestor	This selects all the ancestors (parent, grandparent, and so on) of the element.
descendant	This selects all the descendants (children, grandchildren, and so on) of the element.
following	This selects all elements that follow the closing tab of the current element.
following-sibling	This selects all the siblings after the current element.
parent	This selects the parent of the current element.
preceding	This selects all elements that are before the current element.
preceding-Sibling	This selects all of the siblings before the current element.

As we have seen, there is a large number of different ways to find the same element on the web page. Having XPath queries in your test can be really useful for finding elements on the page, but this can slow down your test. Browsers such as Internet Explorer 6 do not have built-in XPath libraries and rely on doing the XPath query via JavaScript, which can mean that a test that uses XPath can run two or more times slower than a test with IDs. The more complex the XPath, the slower the test since it needs to do more DOM traversals, which is an expensive operation.

There is also another way to do XPath-like queries against the DOM and use built-in libraries in most browsers. We can use CSS selectors, which is explained in the next section of this book.

Working with the XPath axis

Go to `http://financial-dictionary.thefreedictionary.com/` and use `contains()`, `starts-with()` and `ends-with()` on the page. Use the `getXPathCount()` call to see how many items you can get with your XPath query.

CSS selectors

We saw in the previous section that XPath selectors can offer your tests a lot of flexibility to find elements on the page. Here, we will find the elements using CSS selectors (selectors are patterns used to select the elements you want to style.)

> It must be noted that Selenium IDE and Selenium RC use **Sizzle**, the framework used for selectors in jQuery, to find elements on the page. Not all of these can be translated to work in Selenium WebDriver.

Finding elements by CSS

We discussed that finding elements by XPath can be an extremely costly exercise. A way around this is to use CSS selectors to find the objects that you need. Selenium is compatible with CSS 1.0, CSS 2.0, and CSS 3.0 selectors. There are a number of items that are supported, such as namespace in CSS 3.0, and some pseudo classes and pseudo elements.

The syntax of your locator will look like `css=cssSelector`. Let's create our first selector to find an element on our page:

1. Open Selenium IDE.

2. Navigate to `http://book.theautomatedtester.co.uk/chapter2` and click on the Firebug icon. Click on the **Firefinder** tab in Firebug.

3. We will look at one of the buttons in `div` with the ID `divontheleft`. The CSS selector for the buttons will be `div.leftdiv input`. Place that into FireFinder and click on the **Filter** button.

4. Your browser should look something like the following screenshot:

5. Now, if you were to put this into Selenium IDE, insert `css=div.leftdiv input` into the **Target** textbox and click on the **Find** button, it should look like the following screenshot. You can also write this as `div[class='leftdiv']` in Firefinder to make it look similar to XPath:

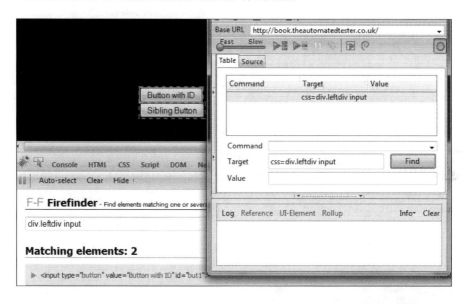

We saw how Selenium has used the same CSS selector to find a button. Unlike in normal CSS, Selenium is only interested in the first element that matches the query, and this is why in the second picture, only the first button was highlighted and not its sibling.

Using child nodes to find the element

In the previous example, we saw that we were able to find the input button that was a child of the `div` node in the DOM. The `div.leftdiv input` will look for `div` and then look for an input node in the DOM that is below it. It looks for any descendant that will match. This is the equivalent to using `descendant` in your XPath query.

If we needed to look for the child of the element, we will have to place > between the `div` selector and the input selector. Your locator will look like `css=div.leftdiv > input` or `css=div.leftdiv input`. In the case of the `Chapter 2` page of the website, both will work as they are direct children of `div.leftdiv`.

Using sibling nodes to find the element

Finding elements by using a sibling node in the DOM is probably the most common way to access an element. In the XPath section of the book, we saw that we can use the `following-sibling` operator in the XPath Query. The equivalent CSS Selector syntax is a + between DOM nodes in the query. It will check its direct next node to see if it matches until it finds the element. So, working against the HTML, we will create a CSS selector to find the second input button:

```
<div id="divontheleft" class="leftdiv">
  <input id='but1' value='Button with ID' type='button'/>
  <br/>
  <input value='Sibling Button' type='button'/>
</div>
```

The `css=input#but1` input will find the first button and then its sibling is `br` and its sibling is `input`. The final selector will look like this:

`css=input#but1 + br + input.`

You can see this in the following screenshot of Selenium IDE:

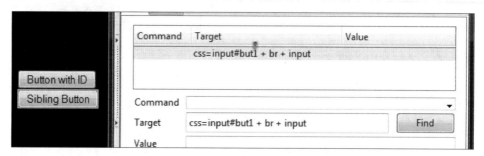

Using CSS class attributes in CSS selectors

Finding elements by their CSS class is probably the most common method. A lot of the queries that people create start with a containing node, distinguishing it by the CSS class, and then moving through the DOM to a child or grandchild node to find the element that you wish to work against. The syntax for finding the item is to use the node, such as `div`, then a dot, and then the class. For example, to find `div` with the `centerdiv` class, it should look like this: `css=div.centerdiv`.

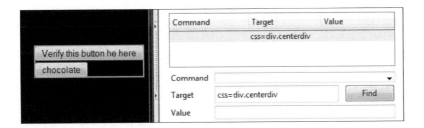

Using element IDs in CSS selectors

As we saw in XPath queries, there are times when we need to find the element that is next to an element for which we know the ID. This means that we can access a lot more of the DOM, and since it is a CSS selector, there is a good chance that it will be a lot faster than its XPath equivalent.

To find an element by ID in a CSS selector, we need to place a # in front of the ID of the element being searched in the CSS selector. For example, if we wanted to find `div` with the ID of `divinthecenter`, the CSS selector will look like this: `css=div#divinthecenter`. You can also simplify this by using `css=#divinthecenter`. This is due to IDs on elements having to be unique.

If you were to place this in the **Target** textbox of Selenium IDE and click **Find**, it should highlight the item, as shown in the following screenshot:

Working with elements and their attributes

In the *Using element attributes in XPath queries* section, we saw how useful it is to find an element by looking at its attributes. An element may have the same name but a different value, so finding its according to its attributes can be extremely powerful.

Finding elements by their attributes

In this example, we will look for the button that has the value `chocolate`. On web page buttons, a value is what is displayed on the screen.

The syntax for looking at the attribute is `node[attribute='value']`. So in the case of the button with the value `chocolate`, it will be `input[value='chocolate']`. If you were to put that into Selenium IDE, it will have the format `css=input[value='chocolate']` and when you click the **Find** button, you will see the same as shown in the following screenshot:

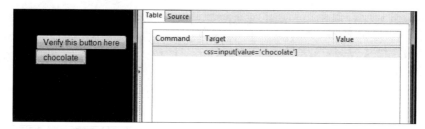

Another example of this is if you were trying to find an element according to its `href`. The syntax for this will be `a[href='path']`. You can try this on the `Index` page and try and find the link to this chapter. When you have done it, it should look something like `css=a[href='/chapter2']`. If you click the **Find** button, it will highlight the `Chapter 2` link.

Chaining of attributes is also supported in Selenium to make sure that your test is using one specific element on the page. The syntax will be `css=node[attr1='value1'][attr2='value2']`. An example on the page that we are working against will be `css=input[id='but1'][value='Button with ID'];`. This will find the button with the value **Button with ID**. You can chain as many attributes as you want in this manner.

Performing partial matches on attributes content

In XPath queries, we saw that we can use `contains` to find partial matches of values to attributes. This can be extremely useful for locating elements based on part of their ID if it is dynamically generated.

The following is a table explaining the different syntax needed to find the CSS, and after this, we will have a look at some working CSS locator examples:

Syntax	Description
`^=`	This finds the item starting with the value passed in. This is the equivalent to the XPath `starts-with`.
`$=`	This finds the item ending with the value passed in. This is the equivalent to the XPath `ends-with`.
`*=`	This finds the item that matches the attribute that has the value that partially matches. This is equivalent to the XPath `contains`.

In the *Finding elements by direct XPath* section of this chapter, we had a look at the XPath `//div[contains(@id,'time_')]`, which has a dynamic ID. The equivalent CSS selector will be `div[id^='time_']` or `div[id*='time_']`. The following screenshot shows both of the selectors highlighting the element we want:

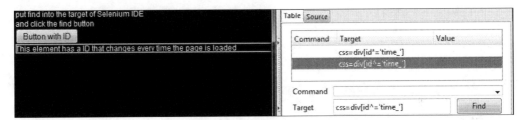

Finding the nth element with CSS

There are times when we need to find the nth element after a parent element on the page. In the XPath examples, we looked at the second input after div with the leftdiv class. The XPath looked like this: xpath=//div[@class='leftdiv']/input[2]. To find the *second* to *nth* element, we will need to use pseudo classes. Pseudo classes are used to add special effects to selectors. In this case, we will use `:nth-child` for the first example:

1. Open Selenium IDE.

2. Navigate to `http://book.theautomatedtester.co.uk/chapter2`.

3. Type `css=div#divinthecenter *:nth-child(3)`. This will find the same element as `xpath=//div[@class='leftdiv']/input[2]`.

4. Click on the Find button.

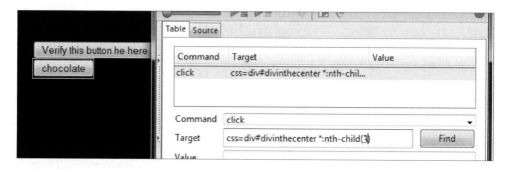

Unfortunately, Selenium does not support the `:nth-of-type` pseudo-class, so you will not be able to access the specific type. This pseudo class is extremely greedy in the way that it does look up over the page. It is also not available to the element selector library that is in use by Selenium. This is why the selector is using the * wildcard and then finding nth-child from our starting div. The downside to using a selector in this manner is, if any other node was placed in the way, it will make the tests fail.

Finding an element by its inner text or partial text

Finding elements by their inner text can also be quite useful. In the XPath section of the book, we used the `text()` function to see the text it had. Earlier, we used `xpath=//div[contains(text(),'element has a ID')]` to find `div` with text in it. To update this XPath to a CSS Selector, we will need to use the :contains pseudo class. This pseudo class is part of Sizzle, which is used in Selenium IDE and Selenium RC. This will only work on browsers that do not have the querySelector CSS available. WebDriver delegates this task down to the browser if it can. I will recommend not using `:contains` if you plan on moving to Selenium WebDriver.

 It is important to know that CSS selectors only have a read forward process. This means that you cannot find an element and then traverse backwards up the DOM. This is what makes CSS selectors a lot faster than XPath queries to find the same elements.

 Now that you have managed to create tests with different locators, try working against Google Maps. It is an extremely good site to work with XPath and CSS as it never has IDs or names.

Summary

We learnt a lot in this chapter about locators. We were able to use a large number of different methods to find the elements that are on a page. We saw how to find elements using easy methods such as `id=`, `name=` to find elements and running queries against the DOM to find them using CSS selectors or XPath queries.

Specifically, we covered the following topics:

- **Using Firebug to find element attributes**: In this section, we were able to start using Firebug. This will become an invaluable tool for anyone who works with web applications. It has a very good mechanism for finding elements so that you can work against them.

- **Finding an element by ID**: Elements can easily be found by the value of the ID attribute. This is the most common way to find elements and is the fastest way to find the elements on the page.

- **Finding an element by name**: When elements do not have IDs but do have a name attribute, your tests can use them.

- **Finding an element by DOM query**: In this section, we were able to use the power of JavaScript DOM API calls to find the element that we wish to work with. This can be from the most basic call to the document to a JavaScript function that you can pass variables to.

- **Finding an element using XPath queries**: In this section, we were able to find the element on the page by using XPath queries. Your test can use relative paths or even XPath functions to find the element on the page. The queries can be as complex as you want, but remember that they can impact the speed of the test.

- **Finding an element using CSS selectors**: When XPath queries slow down your tests, especially in browsers that do not have good support for XPath, CSS selectors are starting to become the default way to find elements on web pages with popular JavaScript libraries, and there is not a large.

We also discussed how XPath queries can make tests run slower on browsers that do not have native XPath support. Microsoft IE is the main browser where you will see this issue. When tests start running extremely slowly with XPath, we can move our tests over to CSS to see large speed gains in our tests.

If a locator does not have a locator type identifier in front of it, Selenium will default to the following strategies:

- **DOM**: For locators starting with a document
- **XPath**: For locators starting with //
- **Identifier**: For any other locator using the ID and name of the element

Now that we've learnt how to locate elements on the page, we're ready to learn how WebDriver is made up, which is the topic of the next chapter.

The summary of locators used in Selenium IDE:

Locators	Description	Example
ID	These elements identify an ID attribute on the page.	`id=inputButton`
Name	These elements identify the name attribute on the page.	`name=buttonFind`
Link	These elements identify links by the text.	`link=index`
XPath	These elements identify by XPath.	`xpath=//div[@ class='classname']`
CSS	These elements identify by CSS.	`css=#divinthecenter`
DOM	These elements identify by DOM.	`dom=document. getElementById("inputButton")`

Self-test questions

1. What color is an element bordered with when the Find button is clicked in Selenium IDE?

    1. Red.

    2. Green.

    3. Amber.

    4. Yellow.

2. If you wanted to use JavaScript to find an element on the page, which strategy would you use to find it?

    1. ID.
    2. Name.
    3. DOM.
    4. CSS Selector.
    5. XPath.

3. Pick two from the following to perform a partial match on an attribute on an element from the beginning of the value:

    1. `contains()`.
    2. `starts-with()`.
    3. `ends-with()`.

4. What is the most common way to find an element on a page?

    1. ID.
    2. XPath.
    3. CSS Selector.
    4. Name.

5. If you wanted to find the sibling input that is after an input in the DOM, what will the XPath look like?

6. What will the CSS look like for the previous question?

3
Overview of the Selenium WebDriver

In this chapter, we will take a look at the history of Selenium WebDriver from its inception to where it currently is. We will also take a look at the architecture of Selenium WebDriver so that we can get a better understanding of how all the commands work. This will help us to take good advantage of the tool and at the same time will help us to construct the right automation framework and use the maximum features of the tool. We will finish the chapter by making sure that we have understood the history of Selenium WebDriver and we will also have a working understanding of how Selenium WebDriver is built.

In this chapter, we will:

- Learn the history of Selenium WebDriver
- Learn about Selenium Architecture
- Set up IDE with IntelliJ IDEA project for Selenium WebDriver
- Set up Eclipse IDE with Java project for Selenium WebDriver and TestNG

So let's get on with it.

In this chapter, we will be writing our tests in Java. This is due to the popularity of the language by people using Selenium as well as its support on multiple platforms. To do this, we will need to have an IDE to write the tests in. You can use IDEA IntelliJ available at `http://www.jetbrains.com/idea/download/` as it will give you all the tools that you need to build your tests successfully. You will also need to download JUnit from `https://github.com/junit-team/junit/wiki/Download-and-Install`. This allows us to drive the tests and perform assertions during the tests.

We are also going to need to download the necessary files that allow us to use Selenium WebDriver with Java. We will need to download `selenium-server-<version>.zip` from `http://code.google.com/p/selenium/downloads/list`. Search for **All Downloads**. The `<version>` will appear like **2.x.x** on the site.

Both Eclipse IDE and IntelliJ are widely used. You can use Eclipse IDE as well as IntelliJ, if you want to try them both.. Eclipse can be downloaded from `http://www.eclipse.org/downloads/`.

History of Selenium

With web applications becoming the de facto approach to developing end user applications, a solution to test is needed. This means more and more emphasis is needed on a browser automation framework to help with checking the site.

For years, people have been using Selenium IDE and Selenium RC to drive a number of different types of browsers. Selenium, when originally created by Jason Huggins, solved the issue of getting the browser to do user interactions.

This is a good automation framework; however, it is limited by the JavaScript sandbox in browsers. The JavaScript sandbox enforces security policies while JavaScript is executing to prevent malicious code executing on the client machine. The main security policy people come across is the Same Origin Policy. If you need to move from HTTP to HTTPS, like you normally would during a log on process, the browser would block the action because we are no longer in the same origin. This was quite infuriating for an average developer!

The Selenium API was originally designed to work from within the server. The developer or tester writing the tests had to do so in HTML using a three column design based on the FIT. You can see how this looks if you open up Selenium IDE: notice the three input boxes that need to be completed for each line that will be executed. Patrick Lightbody and Paul Hammant thought that there must be a better way to drive their tests and in a way that they could use their favorite development language. They created Selenium Remote Control using Java as a web server that would proxy traffic. It would inject Selenium onto the page and then it would be used in a similar way as to the three column manner. This also creates a procedural development style.

The Selenium RC API for the programming languages that are supported has been designed to fit the original three column syntax. Commonly known as Selenese, it has grown over the life of the project to support the changes that have been happening to web applications. This has had the unfortunate consequence that the API has grown organically so that users can manipulate the browser the way they intend, but still keep to the original three column syntax. There are around 140 methods available which makes picking the right method for the job rather difficult.

With the move to mobile devices and HTML5, Selenium RC was starting to show that it wasn't able to fulfill its original requirement: browser automation to mimic what the user is doing.

Simon Stewart, having hit a number of these issues, wanted to try a different approach to driving the browser. While working for ThoughtWorks, he started working on the WebDriver project. It started originally as a way to drive HTMLUnit and Internet Explorer, but having learnt lessons from Selenium RC, Simon was able to design the API to fit in with the way most developers think. Developers have been doing object-orientated development for a while, so moving away from the procedural style of Selenium RC was a welcome change for them. For those interested, I suggest reading Simon Stewart's article on Selenium design at `http://www.aosabook.org/en/selenium.html`.

The next section will go through the basic architecture of WebDriver.

Understanding the WebDriver architecture

The WebDriver architecture does not follow the same approach as Selenium RC (for more details, refer to `http://docs.seleniumhq.org/docs/05_selenium_rc.jsp`), which was written purely in JavaScript for browser automation. The JavaScript, in Selenium RC, would then emulate user actions. This JavaScript would automate the browser from within the browser. On the other hand, WebDriver tries to control the browser from outside the browser. It uses the accessibility API to drive the browser. The accessibility API is used by a number of applications to access and control applications when they are used by disabled users and is common to web browsers.

WebDriver uses the most appropriate way to access the accessibility API. If we look at Firefox, it uses JavaScript to access the API. If we look at Internet Explorer, it uses C++. This approach means that we can control browsers in the best possible way.

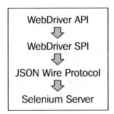

The system is made up of four different layers, as can be seen in the preceding image.

The WebDriver API

The WebDriver API (refer to `http://selenium.googlecode.com/svn/trunk/`
`docs/api/java/index.html?overview-summary.html`) is the part of the system
that you interact with all the time. Things have changed from the 140 line long API
that the Selenium RC API had. This is now more manageable and can actually fit on
a normal screen. This is made up of the WebDriver and the WebElement objects:

```
driver.findElement(By.name("q"))
```

and

```
element.sendKeys("I love cheese");
```

These commands are then translated to the SPI, which is stateless (stateless means
there is no record of previous interactions and each interaction request has to be
handled based entirely on information that comes with it). This can be seen in the
next section.

The WebDriver SPI

When the code enters the **SPI (Stateless Programming Interface)**, it is then
called to a mechanism that breaks down what the element is, using a unique ID,
and then called a command that is relevant. All of the API calls will happen in a
top-down approach.

Using the example in the previous section would be like the following SPI:

```
findElement(using="name", value="q")
sendKeys(element="webdriverID", value="I love cheese")
```

From here, we call the JSON Wire protocol. We still use HTTP as the main transport
mechanism. Developers created the JSON Wire Protocol to communicate with
browsers, a simple client server transport architecture.

The JSON Wire Protocol

The WebDriver developers created a transport mechanism called the **JSON Wire
Protocol**. This protocol is able to transport all the necessary elements to the code
that controls it. It uses a REST-like API as the way to communicate.

The Selenium server

The Selenium server, or browser, depending on what is processing, uses the JSON Wire Protocol commands to break down the JSON object and then does what it needs to. This part of the code is dependent on which browser it is running on.

As mentioned earlier, it could be done in the browser via C++ if it's in IE or if not available, we inject Selenium. Refer to the following screenshot for other language/browser combinations:

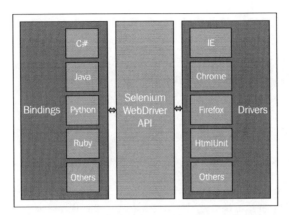

Selenium WebDriver supported languages and browsers

The preceding screenshot shows how many languages the Selenium WebDriver currently supports. In simple words, these are the languages in which we can build the framework, which in turn will interact with the Selenium WebDriver and work on various browsers and other devices. So, we have a common API that we use for Selenium that has a common set of commands and we have various bindings for the different languages. So, you can see there's Java, Python, Ruby; there's also some other bindings and new bindings can be added very easily. The Selenium WebDriver contains a set of common libraries that allow sending commands to respective drivers.

As seen in the screenshot, on the right-hand side, we have the drivers. We have various Internet browser-specific drivers (such as IE driver, Firefox, Chrome), and others such as an HTML unit, which is an interesting one. It works in a headless mode which makes text execution faster. It also contains mobile-specific drivers as well. However, the basic idea here is that each one of these drivers knows how to drive the browser that it corresponds to. So, the Chrome driver knows how to handle the low level details of the Chrome browser and drives it to do things, such as clicking a button, going into pages, getting data from the browser itself; the same thing goes for Firefox, IE, and so on.

Merging of two projects

Both Simon Stewart and Jason Huggins thought that it would be a really good idea to merge the two projects together. This was then called **Selenium 2**.

The Selenium core developers have been working really hard to simplify the code base and remove as much duplication as possible. We have created what is known as **Selenium Atoms**, which is then shared between the two projects.

Now that we know the basics of how it all hangs together, let's set up a project that we can use for the rest of the chapter. By performing the steps in the link given below, we would be able to set up our Java environment:

1. Install JDK 1.6 or higher from the Oracle website: `http://www.oracle.com/technetwork/java/javase/downloads/index.html`.

2. To set up Java environment, refer to `http://www.tutorialspoint.com/java/java_environment_setup.htm`.

Setting up the IntelliJ IDEA project

We will be setting up IntelliJ IDEA project using JUnit as the testing framework to drive our tests. Let's get started with the following steps:

1. Open IDEA and create a new project:

2. Create a directory at the root of the project called `test` using **New | Directory**:

3. Click on **File | Project structure**.
4. Click on **Modules** on the left-hand side of the dialog box that has loaded.

5. Click on the `test` folder that you created in the folder tree on the right-hand side of the dialog box:

6. Click on the **Test Sources** button and the `test` folder should turn green. It will look like the following screenshot:

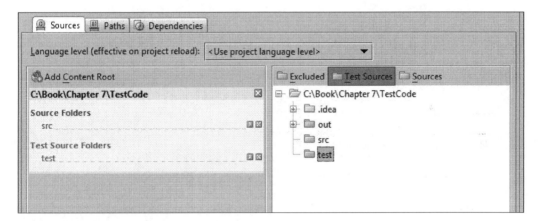

7. Click on **File | Project structure**.

8. Then, click on **Global libraries**.

9. Click on the **+** button to add a **New Global library**. Then, select **Java**.

10. Click on **Attach Classes** and add `selenium.jar` and `common.jar`. This should be in the same place as your `Selenium-Server.jar`. When added, it should look like the following screenshot:

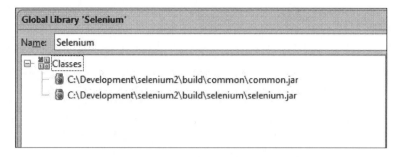

11. Do the same for JUnit now. You can create a **New Global library** for it or add it to the **Selenium Global Library**.

12. Click on the **Modules** link on the left-hand side again.

13. Click on the **Dependencies** tab.

14. Click on **Add** and then click on **Global Libraries**. Add the Selenium and JUnit libraries.

15. Click on **Apply**.

16. We are now ready to run Selenium Server. We do this by running `java-jar selenium-server.jar` from Command Prompt or from a terminal, depending on your operating system.

Your project is ready to have tests added to it. Each of the files that we create from now on will be placed in the test directory and can be run when we need to.

Setting up Eclipse IDE with Java project for Selenium WebDriver and TestNG

Here is a step by step explanation of setting up Eclipse IDE with Java project for the Selenium WebDriver and TestNG.

Downloading WebDriver JAR files

Download the Selenium WebDriver language bindings from `http://docs.seleniumhq.org/download/`. Unzip the downloaded Selenium WebDriver file; it will create a folder containing the Selenium WebDriver JAR files.

Downloading and installing Eclipse

Based on your system configuration type (32 bit or 64 bit), download the Eclipse IDE for the Java EE Developers Edition from `http://www.eclipse.org/downloads/packages/release/Mars/M3`. Save the file, as it is about to download somewhere on your disk drive. The exact form of this interaction will depend on which operating system you are using. Store this `zip` file somewhere permanent on your disk drive so that you can unzip it (recreate Eclipse) later, if necessary.

Following are the steps that will install Eclipse on Windows:

1. Unzip the file that you just downloaded. It creates a folder named `Eclipse`. You can leave this folder here or move it elsewhere on your disk drive.

2. Create a shortcut on your desktop to the `eclipse.exe` file. Now, you are ready to perform a one-time only setup of Eclipse.

3. Double-click on the shortcut to Eclipse that you just created. In the Workspace Launcher window, in the box following Workspace should appear something like `C:\Documents and Settings\username\workspace` (where *username* is your login name on the machine). If you want, you can type in (or browse) another location for the workspace file to be created, but I advise accepting the default.

4. In the Eclipse IDE, open the **File** menu, select **New** and **Java Project** to create a new project.

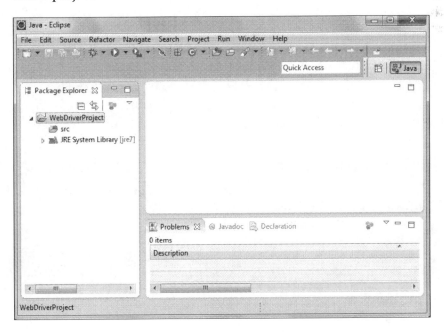

Configuring WebDriver with Eclipse

In the **Package Explorer** window, right-click on created project, select **Build Path** and **Configure Build path…**. The Java Build Path dialogue box appears. Click on the **Add External Jars…** button and choose the location where all your Selenium WebDriver JAR files are stored. Then click on **OK** on the Java Build Path dialogue box. Refer to the following screenshot in the Package Explorer window; you can see Referenced Libraries added to a project. This is how you need to configure the Selenium WebDriver to Eclipse:

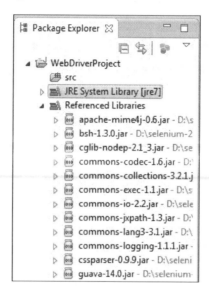

TestNG plug-in installation for Eclipse

There is no need to download any JAR or .exe file for installation. We just need to utilize the **Install New Software** option available in Eclipse.

Steps for installation

1. Open Eclipse IDE, then click on **Help** on the menu bar and select **Install New Software**. The **Install** dialogue box appears.

2. Type `http://beust.com/eclipse` in the **Work with** edit box. In the **Name** column, you can see **TestNG**. Click on the **TestNG** checkbox, and then click on the **Next** button:

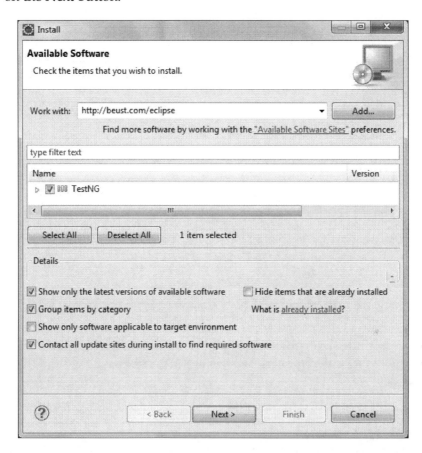

3. The **Install** dialogue box appears; select **TestNG** from the listed **Name** tab and click on the **Next** button. Click on the **I accept the terms of the license agreement** radio button and click on the **Finish** button.

This will install the TestNG plugin for Eclipse. After the installation, it will ask to restart Eclipse. Click on the **Yes** button. Once Eclipse is restarted, TestNG should be installed. To confirm whether it is installed successfully, first select the project, then click on **Run** from the Eclipse menu bar, and select the **Run As** option from the drop-down list. Here, you should be able to see **TestNG Test**. Refer to the following screenshot for the same:

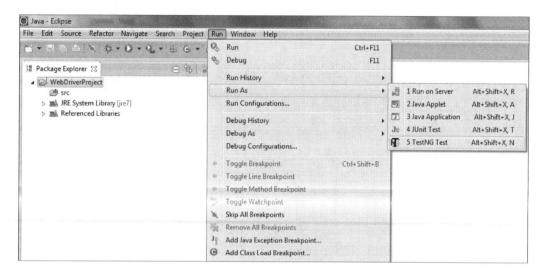

We have successfully set up a project in the Selenium WebDriver. When we are working through the next chapters, we will know that they will have all the aspects that are needed.

Summary

You learned a lot in this chapter about how Selenium and WebDriver were created and how they work together.

Specifically, we covered:

- **History**: In this section, you learned how Selenium came into being. Selenium WebDriver is the merger of two automation frameworks: Selenium and WebDriver.

- **Architecture**: You learned how all of the different mechanisms work together to produce the framework that we will be using throughout this book.

- **Setting up a Java environment**: In this section, you learned how you can run projects later on in the book.

- **Setting up IDE IntelliJ IDEA project**: In this section, you learned how the project is created in IDE and how the Selenium JAR files can be associated in the project.
- **Setting up Eclipse IDE**: Configure WebDriver and TestNG with Eclipse.

Now that you've learned the history and architecture of the Selenium WebDriver, as well as setting up your environment to create Java projects, we will have a look at the design patterns we should use with the Selenium WebDriver to make test creation easier, which is the topic of the next chapter.

Self-test questions

1. Selenium WebDriver supports multiple programming languages?

    a. True

    b. False

2. Selenium WebDriver supports multiple browsers?

    a. True

    b. False

3. Selenium WebDriver requires a browser-specific driver to support the different browsers?

    a. True

    b. False

4. In Eclipse, where do you find Selenium JAR files?

    a. JRE System Library

    b. Referenced Libraries

    c. Source folder

    d. None of the above

5. To work on Eclipse, we need to have workspace created?

    a. True

    b. False

4
Finding Elements

In this chapter, we will look at how to find elements on the page using the WebDriver API. One of the things that we learned in the previous chapter was that WebDriver and its architecture have a major component called **driver**. This has the commands to find elements.

Let's start with the different commands. We begin with the helper commands and then move on to the more generic commands, which take different types of objects. We will finish the chapter with some helpful techniques when interacting with element finding.

Two major learning points are as follows:

- Finding elements on the page by their ID, name, ClassName, XPath, and link list
- Tips to use find element calls

So let's get on with it. When working with the following examples, we are going to assume that you have instantiated a WebDriver object by using the following code:

```
WebDriver driver = new FirefoxDriver();
```

You can use the following example class with TestNG. The test is a stub that we can use throughout the chapter:

```
import org.openqa.selenium.*;
import org.openqa.selenium.firefox.*;
import org.testng.annotations.*;


public class TestExample1 {

  Webdriver driver;
```

```
@BeforeTest
public void setUp(){
  driver = new FirefoxDriver();
  driver.get("http://book.theautomatedtester.co.uk/chapter1");
}

@AfterTest
public void tearDown(){
  driver.quit();
}

@Test
public void testExamples(){
  // We will put examples in here
}
}
```

We should also note that finding elements can be achieved from an element. For example, if we wanted to find the first (Child) link after a called button (parent), we would write something like the following code:

```
// Get the webelement of a parent - Button
WebElement element = ((FindsById)driver).findElementById("button");
// Get the webelement of a Clild - Link
WebElement childElement = element.findElement(By.tagName("a"));
```

We will look at what this means in-depth as we go through the chapter.

Finding elements

When working with WebDriver on a web application, we will need to find elements on the page. This is the core to being able to work. All the methods to perform actions on the web application (such as typing and clicking) require searching the element first.

Finding an element on the page by its ID

The first item that we will look at is finding an element by ID. Finding elements by ID is one of the easiest ways to do this. We will start with findElementByID(). This method is a helper method that sets an argument for a more generic findElement call. We will see now how we can use it in action. The method's signature looks like the following code:

```
findElementById(String using);
```

The `using` variable takes the ID of the element that you wish to look for. It will return a `WebElement` object that we can then work with.

Using findElementById()

We will find an element on the page using the `findElementById()` method that is on each of the browser driver classes. The `findElement` calls will return a `WebElement` object that we can perform actions on.

Follow these steps to see how it works:

1. Open your Java IDE (IntelliJ or Eclipse are the ones that are mostly used).

2. Use the following command:

    ```
    WebElement element = ((FindsById)driver).
        findElementById("verifybutton");
    ```

3. Run the test from the IDE. It will look like the following screenshot:

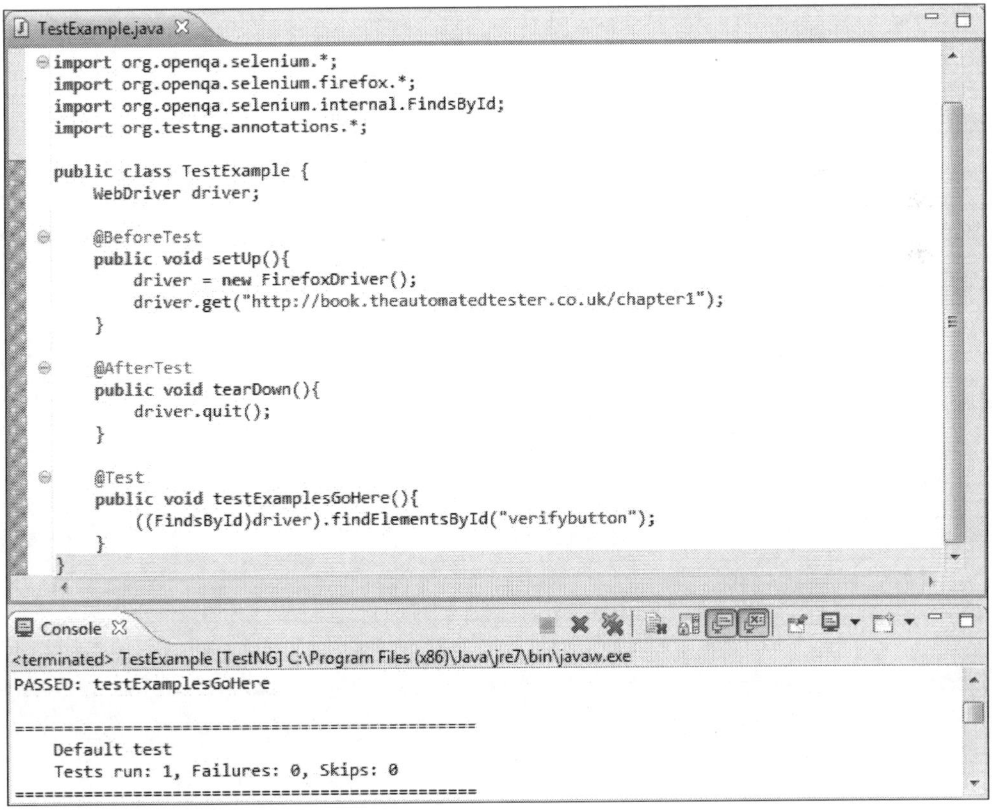

```java
import org.openqa.selenium.*;
import org.openqa.selenium.firefox.*;
import org.openqa.selenium.internal.FindsById;
import org.testng.annotations.*;

public class TestExample {
    WebDriver driver;

    @BeforeTest
    public void setUp(){
        driver = new FirefoxDriver();
        driver.get("http://book.theautomatedtester.co.uk/chapter1");
    }

    @AfterTest
    public void tearDown(){
        driver.quit();
    }

    @Test
    public void testExamplesGoHere(){
        ((FindsById)driver).findElementsById("verifybutton");
    }
}
```

```
Console
<terminated> TestExample [TestNG] C:\Program Files (x86)\Java\jre7\bin\javaw.exe
PASSED: testExamplesGoHere

===============================================
    Default test
    Tests run: 1, Failures: 0, Skips: 0
===============================================
```

We have just seen how we can find an element using the `findElementById` helper method. After running the test, we saw that it passed. This means that it found the element. If an element is not found in Selenium, WebDriver will throw a `NoSuchElementFoundException` exception.

Finding elements on the page by their ID

In addition to `findElementById`, there is `findElementsByID`. This call has been added to the API so that there is some symmetry in the API although it's against the HTML specification to have more than one item in the DOM with an ID. We will now see how we can use it in action. The method's signature looks like this:

```
findElementsById(String using);
```

The `using` variable takes the ID of the element that you wish to look for. It will return a `WebElement` object that we can then work with.

Using findElementsById()

We are going to find an element on the page using the `findElementsById()` method that is on each of the browser driver classes. The `findElement` calls return a `WebElement` object that we can perform actions on.

Follow these steps to see how it works:

1. Open your Java IDE.
2. Use this command:

```
List<WebElement> elements = ((FindsById)driver)
  .findElementsById("verifybutton");
Assert.assertEquals(1, elements.size());
```

3. Run the test from the IDE. It will look like the following screenshot:

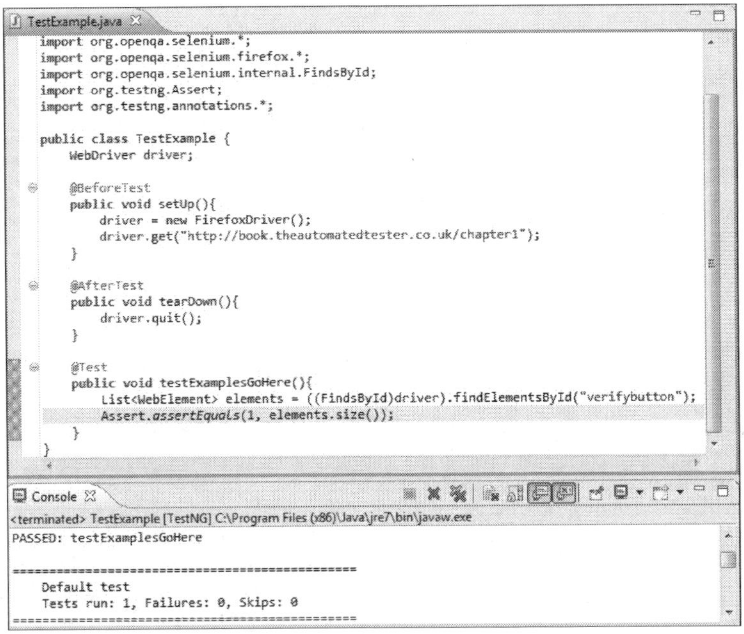

We have just seen how we can find an element using the `findElementsById` helper method. After running the test, we saw that it passed. Unlike its singular version, it will not throw a `NoSuchElementException` exception if the element is not found. It will return a list that has a size of zero.

Finding an element on the page by its name

The next item that we will look at is finding an element by its name. Finding elements by name is just as fast as by using their equivalent ID. This method is a helper method that sets an argument for a more generic `findElement` call. We will now see how we can use it. The method's signature looks like the following code:

```
findElementByName(String using);
```

The `using` variable takes the ID of the element that you wish to look for. It will return a `WebElement` object that we can then work with.

Using findElementByName()

Let's find an element on the page using the `findElementByName()` method that is on each of the Browser Driver classes. The `findElement` calls return a `WebElement` object that we can perform actions on.

Follow these steps to see how it works:

1. Open your Java IDE.

2. Use the following command:

```
WebElement element = ((FindsByName)driver).
    findElementByName("selected(1234)");
```

3. Run the test from the IDE. It will look like the following screenshot:

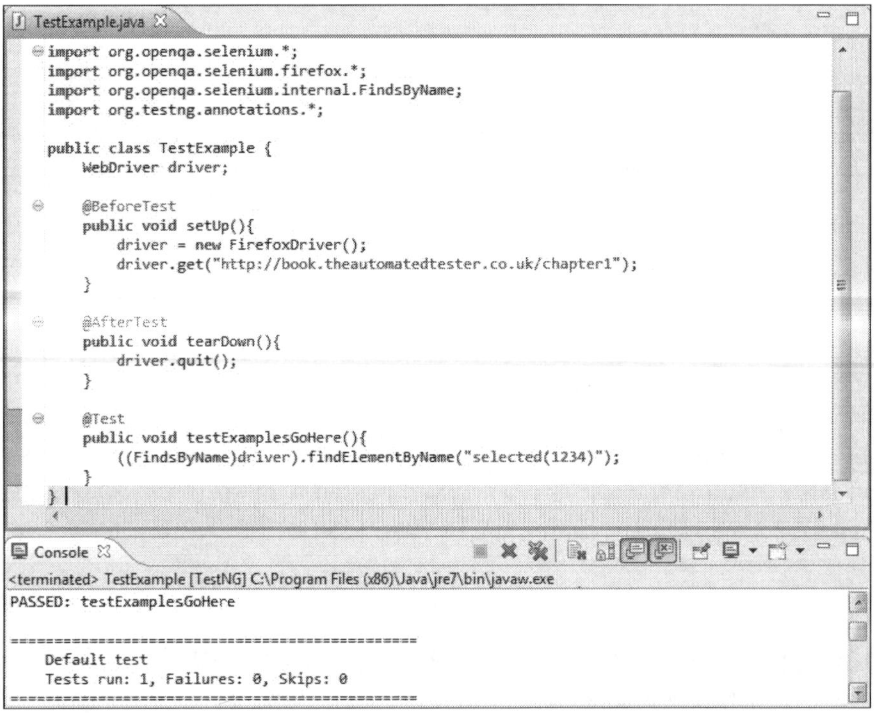

```
TestExample.java ⊠
import org.openqa.selenium.*;
import org.openqa.selenium.firefox.*;
import org.openqa.selenium.internal.FindsByName;
import org.testng.annotations.*;

public class TestExample {
    WebDriver driver;

    @BeforeTest
    public void setUp(){
        driver = new FirefoxDriver();
        driver.get("http://book.theautomatedtester.co.uk/chapter1");
    }

    @AfterTest
    public void tearDown(){
        driver.quit();
    }

    @Test
    public void testExamplesGoHere(){
        ((FindsByName)driver).findElementByName("selected(1234)");
    }
}
```

```
Console ⊠
<terminated> TestExample [TestNG] C:\Program Files (x86)\Java\jre7\bin\javaw.exe
PASSED: testExamplesGoHere


===========================================
    Default test
    Tests run: 1, Failures: 0, Skips: 0
===========================================
```

We have just seen how we can find an element using the `findElementByName` helper method. After running the test, we saw that it passed. This means that it found the element. If an element is not found in Selenium, WebDriver will throw a `NotSuchElementFound` exception.

Finding elements on the page by their name

Unlike with ID, we can have multiple elements on the page with the same name. This is also a symmetrical call to find multiple elements. We will now see how we can use it in action. The method's signature looks like:

```
findElementsByName(String using);
```

The `using` variable takes the ID of the element that you wish to look for. It will return a `WebElement` object that we can then work with.

Using findElementsByName()

Let's find an element on the page using the `findElementsByName()` method that is on each of the browser driver classes. The `findElement` call returns a list of `WebElement` objects that we can perform actions on.

Follow these steps to see how it works:

1. Open your Java IDE.

2. Use this command:

```
List<WebElement> elements = ((FindsByName)driver).
    findElementsByName("selected(1234)");
Assert.assertEquals(1, elements.size());
```

3. Run the test from the IDE. It will look like the following screenshot:

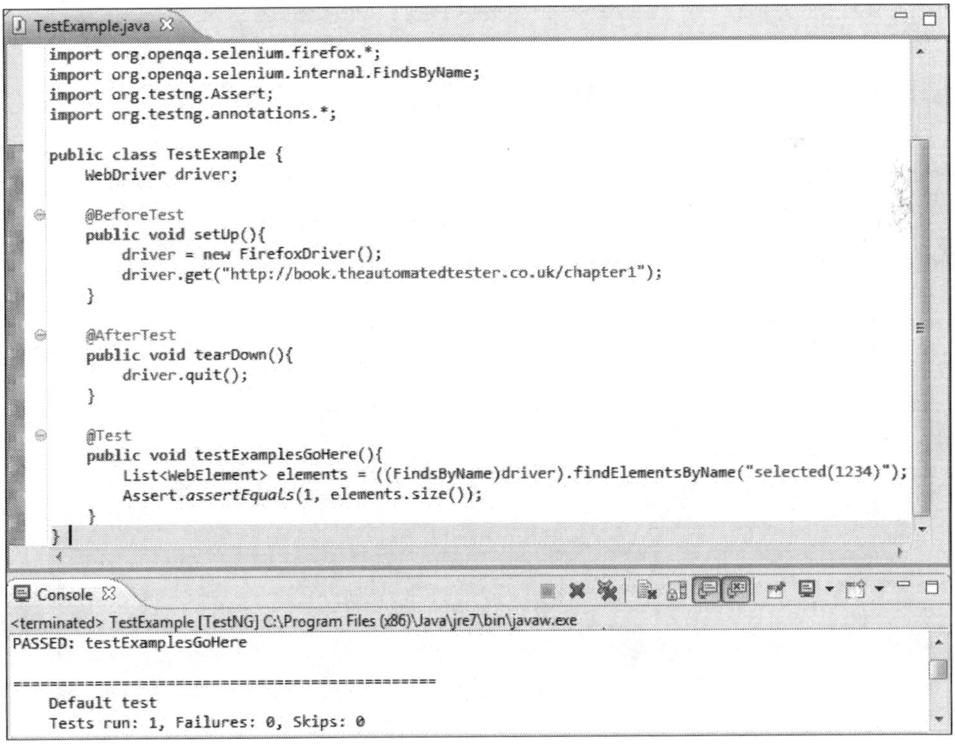

```
import org.openqa.selenium.firefox.*;
import org.openqa.selenium.internal.FindsByName;
import org.testng.Assert;
import org.testng.annotations.*;

public class TestExample {
    WebDriver driver;

    @BeforeTest
    public void setUp(){
        driver = new FirefoxDriver();
        driver.get("http://book.theautomatedtester.co.uk/chapter1");
    }

    @AfterTest
    public void tearDown(){
        driver.quit();
    }

    @Test
    public void testExamplesGoHere(){
        List<WebElement> elements = ((FindsByName)driver).findElementsByName("selected(1234)");
        Assert.assertEquals(1, elements.size());
    }
}
```

```
Console
<terminated> TestExample [TestNG] C:\Program Files (x86)\Java\jre7\bin\javaw.exe
PASSED: testExamplesGoHere

===============================================
    Default test
    Tests run: 1, Failures: 0, Skips: 0
```

We have just seen how we can find an element using the `findElementsByName` helper method. After running the test, we saw that it passed. Unlike its singular version, it will not throw `NoSuchElementException` if the element is not found. It will return a list that has a size of zero.

Finding an element on the page by its ClassName

We will now look at `findElementByClassName()`. If there is more than one element on the page that has this class name, then it will return the first element that it gets.

We will now see how we can use it in action. The method's signature looks like the following code:

```
findElementByClassName(String using);
```

The `using` variable takes the ID of the element that you wish to look for. It will return a `WebElement` object that we can then work with.

Using findElementByClassName()

We are going to find an element on the page using the `findElementByClassName()` method that is on each of the browser driver classes. The `findElement` calls return a `WebElement` object that we can perform actions on.

Follow these steps to see how it works:

1. Open your Java IDE.

2. Use this command:

```
WebElement element = ((FindsByClassName)driver).
    findElementByClassName("storetext");
```

3. Run the test from the IDE. It will look like the following screenshot:

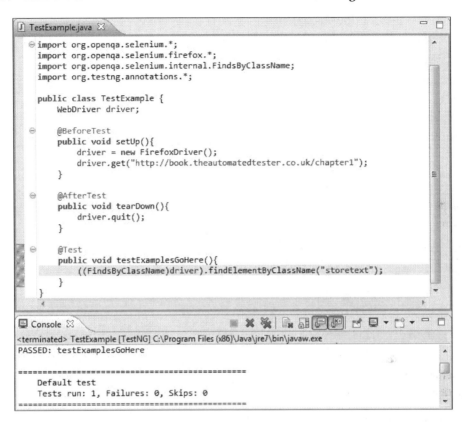

We have just seen how we can find an element using the `findElementByClassName` helper method. After running the test, we saw that it passed. This means that it found the element. If an element is not found in Selenium, WebDriver will throw a `NotSuchElementFound` exception.

Finding elements on the page by their ClassName

We will now see how we can use it in action. The method's signature looks like:

```
findElementsByClass(String using);
```

The `using` variable takes the ID of the element that you wish to look for. It will return a `WebElement` object that we can then work with.

Using findElementsByClassName()

Let's find an element on the page using the `findElementByClassName()` method that is on each of the Browser Driver classes. The `findElement` calls will return a `WebElement` object that we can perform actions on.

Follow these steps to see it work:

1. Open your Java IDE.

2. Use the following command:

   ```
   List<WebElement> elements = ((FindsByClassName)driver)
     .findElementsByClassName("storetext");
   Assert.assertEquals(1, elements.size());
   ```

3. Run the test from the IDE. It will look like the following screenshot:

```
TestExample.java

    import org.openqa.selenium.firefox.*;
    import org.openqa.selenium.internal.FindsByClassName;
    import org.testng.Assert;
    import org.testng.annotations.*;

    public class TestExample {
        WebDriver driver;

        @BeforeTest
        public void setUp(){
            driver = new FirefoxDriver();
            driver.get("http://book.theautomatedtester.co.uk/chapter1");
        }

        @AfterTest
        public void tearDown(){
            driver.quit();
        }

        @Test
        public void testExamplesGoHere(){
            List<WebElement> elements = ((FindsByClassName)driver).findElementsByClassName("storetext");
            Assert.assertEquals(1, elements.size());
        }
    }
```

```
Console
<terminated> TestExample [TestNG] C:\Program Files (x86)\Java\jre7\bin\javaw.exe
PASSED: testExamplesGoHere

===================================================
    Default test
    Tests run: 1, Failures: 0, Skips: 0
```

We have just seen how we can find an element using the `findElementsByClassName` helper method. After running the test, we saw that it passed. Unlike its singular version, it will not throw `NoSuchElementException` if the element is not found. It will return a list that has a size of zero. If you want to use CSS selectors, you can use `findElementByCssSelector` or `findElementsByCssSelector`. In the next section, we will take a look at XPath expressions.

Finding an element on the page by its XPath

XPath is one of the most useful approaches to find elements on the page. It has a bit of a tainted past due to the speed it takes to look up elements on the page. We learned a number of different techniques using XPath in *Chapter 3, Overview of the Selenium WebDriver*.

This method is a helper method that sets an argument for a more generic `findElement` call. We will now see how we can use it in action. The method's signature looks like the following code:

```
findElementByXpath(String using);
```

The using variable takes the ID of the element that you wish to look for. It will return a `WebElement` object that we can then work with.

Using findElementByXPath()

Let's find an element on the page using the `findElementByXPath()` method that is on each of the browser driver classes. The `findElement` calls return a `WebElement` object that we can perform actions on.

Follow these steps to see it work:

1. Open your Java IDE.

2. Use the following command:

```
WebElement element = ((FindsByXPath)driver).
    findElementByXPath("//input[@id='verifybutton']");
```

3.   Run the test from the IDE. It will look like the following screenshot:

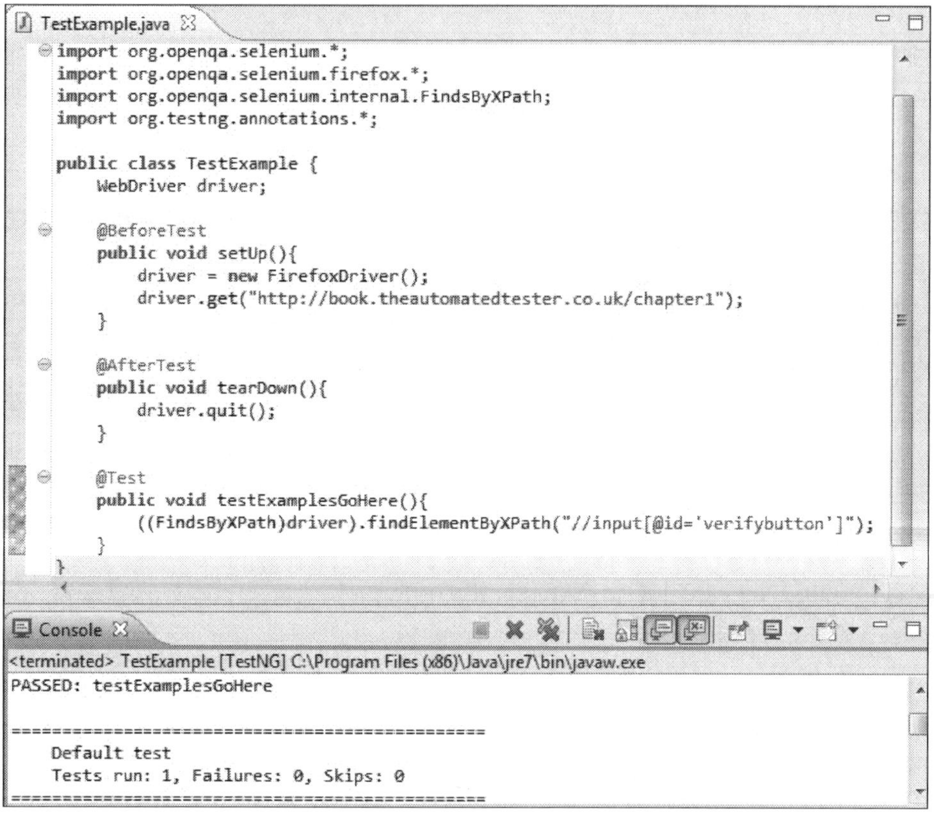

```
TestExample.java ⌧
  import org.openqa.selenium.*;
  import org.openqa.selenium.firefox.*;
  import org.openqa.selenium.internal.FindsByXPath;
  import org.testng.annotations.*;

  public class TestExample {
      WebDriver driver;

      @BeforeTest
      public void setUp(){
          driver = new FirefoxDriver();
          driver.get("http://book.theautomatedtester.co.uk/chapter1");
      }

      @AfterTest
      public void tearDown(){
          driver.quit();
      }

      @Test
      public void testExamplesGoHere(){
          ((FindsByXPath)driver).findElementByXPath("//input[@id='verifybutton']");
      }
  }
```

```
Console ⌧
<terminated> TestExample [TestNG] C:\Program Files (x86)\Java\jre7\bin\javaw.exe
PASSED: testExamplesGoHere

===============================================
    Default test
    Tests run: 1, Failures: 0, Skips: 0
===============================================
```

We have just seen how we can find an element using the findElementByXPath helper method. After running the test in XPath, we saw that the test has passed. If an element is not found in Selenium, WebDriver will throw a NotSuchElementFound exception.

Finding elements on the page by their XPath

We will now see how we can use it in action. The method's signature looks like this:

```
findElementsByXPath(String using);
```

The using variable takes the ID of the element that you wish to look for. It will return a WebElement object that we can then work with.

Using findElementsByXpath()

Let's find an element on the page using the `findElementsByXPath()` method that is on each of the Browser Driver classes. The `findElement` calls will return a `WebElement` object that we can perform actions on.

Follow these steps to see it work:

1. Open your Java IDE.

2. Use the following command:

```
List<WebElement> elements = ((FindsByXPath)driver).
    findElementsByXPath("//input");
Assert.equals(5, elements.size());
```

3. Run the test from the IDE. It will look like the following screenshot:

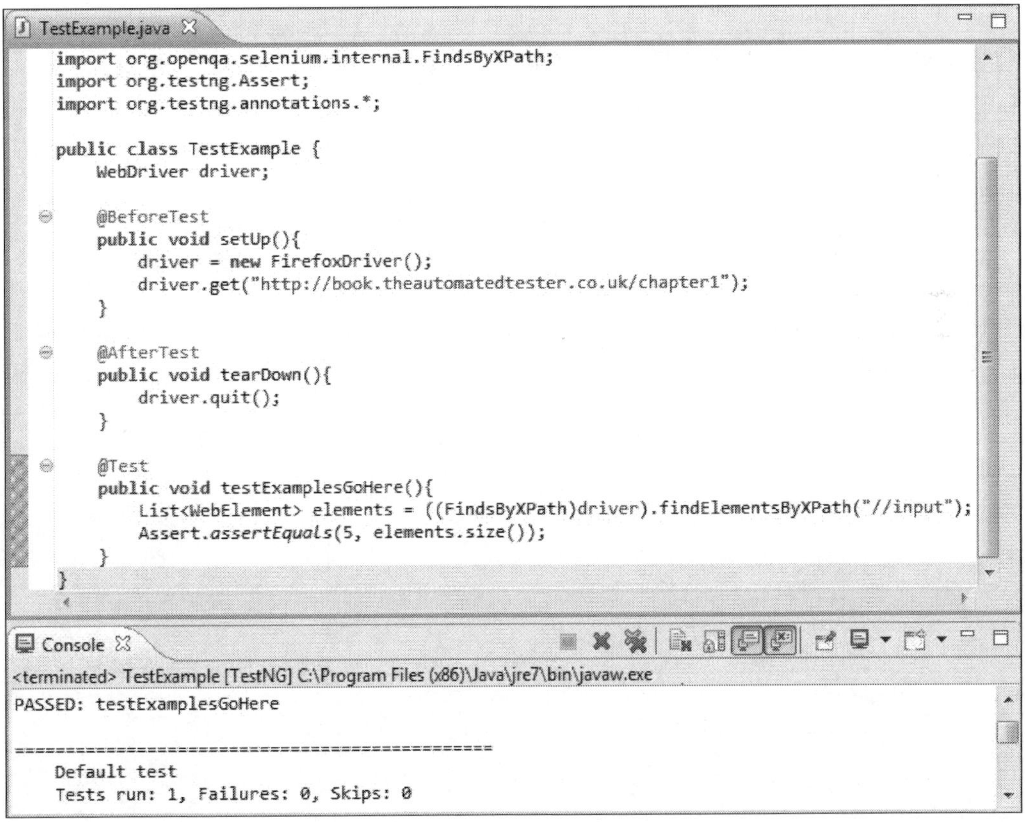

```
import org.openqa.selenium.internal.FindsByXPath;
import org.testng.Assert;
import org.testng.annotations.*;

public class TestExample {
    WebDriver driver;

    @BeforeTest
    public void setUp(){
        driver = new FirefoxDriver();
        driver.get("http://book.theautomatedtester.co.uk/chapter1");
    }

    @AfterTest
    public void tearDown(){
        driver.quit();
    }

    @Test
    public void testExamplesGoHere(){
        List<WebElement> elements = ((FindsByXPath)driver).findElementsByXPath("//input");
        Assert.assertEquals(5, elements.size());
    }
}
```

```
Console ⊠                                      ■ ✖ ✖ | ■ ■ ■ ■ ■ | ■ ■ ▼ ■ ▼ ▭ ■
<terminated> TestExample [TestNG] C:\Program Files (x86)\Java\jre7\bin\javaw.exe
PASSED: testExamplesGoHere

===============================================
    Default test
    Tests run: 1, Failures: 0, Skips: 0
```

We have just seen how we can find an element using the `findElementsByXPath` helper method. After running the test, we saw that it passed. Unlike its singular version, it will not throw a `NoSuchElement` exception if the element is not found. It will return a list that has a size of zero.

Finding an element on the page by its link text

If you need to find a link by the text that is in it, this method is useful. It is a helper method that sets an argument for a more generic `findElement` call. We will now see how we can use it in action. The method's signature looks like this:

```
findElementByLinkText(String using);
```

The using variable takes the link text of the element that you wish to look for. It will return a `WebElement` object that we can then work with.

Using findElementByLinkText()

Let's find an element on the page using the `findElementByLinkText()` method that is on each of the browser driver classes. The `findElement` calls will return a `WebElement` object that we can perform actions on.

Follow these steps to see it work:

1. Open your Java IDE.

2. Use the following command. For this example, we'll use a different page on the site:

```
Driver.get("http://book.theautomatedtester.co.uk")
WebElement element = ((FindsByLinkText)driver).
  findElementByLinkText("Chapter1");
```

3. Run the test from the IDE. It will look like the following screenshot:

```
TestExample.java ×
import org.openqa.selenium.*;
import org.openqa.selenium.firefox.*;
import org.openqa.selenium.internal.FindsByLinkText;
import org.testng.annotations.*;

public class TestExample {
    WebDriver driver;

    @BeforeTest
    public void setUp(){
        driver = new FirefoxDriver();
        driver.get("http://book.theautomatedtester.co.uk/");
    }

    @AfterTest
    public void tearDown(){
        driver.quit();
    }

    @Test
    public void testExamplesGoHere(){
        ((FindsByLinkText)driver).findElementByLinkText("Chapter1");
    }
}
```

```
Console ×
<terminated> TestExample [TestNG] C:\Program Files (x86)\Java\jre7\bin\javaw.exe
PASSED: testExamplesGoHere

=================================================
    Default test
    Tests run: 1, Failures: 0, Skips: 0
```

We have just seen how we can find an element using the `findElementByLinkText` helper method. One thing to note here is that the search for the text is case sensitive when used in WebDriver. This means that WebDriver needs to match exactly what we pass into Selenium, or it will not find your element. If an element is not found in Selenium, WebDriver will throw a `NoSuchElementFound` exception.

Finding elements on the page by their link text

We will now see how we can find elements on the page with its link text in action. The method's signature looks like this:

```
findElementsByLinkText(String using);
```

The `using` variable takes the link text of the element that you wish to look for. It will return a `WebElement` object that we can then work with.

Using findElementsByLinkText()

Let's find an element on the page using the `findElementsByLinkText()` method that is on each of the browser driver classes. The `findElements` calls will return a list of `WebElement` objects that we can perform actions on.

Follow these steps to see it work:

1. Open your Java IDE.

2. Use the following command:

```
driver.get("http://book.theautomatedtester.co.uk")
List<WebElement> elements = ((FindsByLinkText)driver).
    findElementsByLinkText("Chapter1");
Assert.equals(1, elements.size());
```

3. Run the test from the IDE. It will look like the following screenshot:

```
TestExample.java

import org.openqa.selenium.internal.FindsByLinkText;
import org.testng.Assert;
import org.testng.annotations.*;

public class TestExample {
    WebDriver driver;

    @BeforeTest
    public void setUp(){
        driver = new FirefoxDriver();
        driver.get("http://book.theautomatedtester.co.uk/");
    }

    @AfterTest
    public void tearDown(){
        driver.quit();
    }

    @Test
    public void testExamplesGoHere(){
        List<WebElement> elements = ((FindsByLinkText)driver).findElementsByLinkText("Chapter1");
        Assert.assertEquals(1, elements.size());
    }
}
```

```
Console
<terminated> TestExample [TestNG] C:\Program Files (x86)\Java\jre7\bin\javaw.exe
PASSED: testExamplesGoHere

=================================================
Default test
  Tests run: 1, Failures: 0, Skips: 0
```

We have just seen how we can find an element using the `findElementsByLinkText` helper method. One thing to note here is that the search for the text is case sensitive. If an element is not found in Selenium, WebDriver will return an empty list.

Using findElement Helper methods

Let's try to create an example where you need to find an element using the CSS selector. This is used by `findElementByCssSelector` and `findElementsByCssSelector`.

For example,

using `indElementByCssSelector`:

```
Driver.get("http://book.theautomatedtester.co.uk")
WebElement element = ((FindsByCssSelector)driver).
    findElementByCssSelector("Chapter1");
```

using `findElementsByCssSelector`:

```
driver.get("http://book.theautomatedtester.co.uk")
List<WebElement> elements = ((FindsByCssSelector)driver).
    findElementsByCssSelector("Chapter1");
Assert.equals(1, elements.size());
```

Finding elements using a more generic method

We have had a look at using helper methods to find elements on the page. The downside to this is that, if something changes, you need to change the entire method that you are using to find the element. This can increase maintenance costs.

The other approach is to use the `findElement()` method, pass in the `By` abstract class, and call static methods on this class.

Let's see this in action.

Using findElement()

In this section, we will look at using the `findElement` call that is on the WebDriver object. This is how we normally find elements using Selenium WebDriver:

1. Open your Java IDE.
2. Use the following command:
    ```
    driver.get("http://book.theautomatedtester.co.uk")
    driver.findElement(By.linkText("Chapter1"));
    ```
3. Run your test.

We have just seen that we can find an element by passing in the `By` object. This is a static class that gives people a mechanism to find elements, as we did earlier in the chapter. This will throw `NoSuchElementException` if it cannot find the element.

Let's now have a look at how to find multiple elements.

Using findElements()

In this section, we will take a look at how to use the `findElements` call that is on the WebDriver object. This is how we normally find elements using Selenium WebDriver:

1. Open your Java IDE.

2. Use this command:

```
driver.get("http://book.theautomatedtester.co.uk")
List<WebElement> elements =  driver.findElements(
  By.linkText("Chapter1"));
Assert.assertEquals(1, elements.size());
```

3. Run your test.

We used a similar call earlier in the *Using findElementsByLinkText()* section. This will search multiple elements on the page and returns a list. It will not throw a `NoSuchElement` exception if it cannot find the element.

Tips and tricks

In this section, we will take a look at some tips and tricks that might be of use when trying to find elements on the page. We can also apply them to see whether the elements are not on the page.

Finding if an element exists without throwing an error

Selenium WebDriver is really good at letting you know when an element does not exist. If it throws `NoSuchElementException`, then we know it's not there. Unfortunately, I, and many others, are not big fans of using exception handling as a means of flow control.

To get around this, we can use the `findElements()` call, and then we just need to check that the size of the list returned is `0`. For example:

```
List<WebElement> elements = driver.findElements(
   By.Id("myElement"));
elements.size(); //This should be zero and can be checked accordingly
```

Waiting for elements to appear on the page

Web applications now want to appear as though they are desktop applications as more and more people move to hardware, such as tablets or netbooks, which have very small hard drives. This is all done through AJAX to the page.

This means that when we are working with Selenium WebDriver, we need to have it synchronized with what is happening on the page. We do not want to use something like `Thread.sleep()` because this doesn't make our tests run as quickly as possible. We need to use one of the next two approaches: **implicit** or **explicit** waits.

Implicit waits

Selenium WebDriver borrowed the idea of implicit waits from `Watir`. This means that we can tell Selenium that we would like it to wait until the particular element appears for a certain amount of time. If it cannot find the element on the page, then throws an exception. We should note that implicit waits will be in place for the entire time the browser is open. This means that any search for elements on the page could take the time the implicit wait is set for. Let's see how we can use this.

Using implicit waits

In this section, we will see how we can use implicit waits in our code. We need to change a number of calls together to set to implicit. This is done to keep the API as succinct as possible:

1. Open your Java IDE.
2. Use the following command:

```
driver.manage().timeouts().implicitlyWait(10, TimeUnit.SECONDS);
driver.findElement(By.xpath("//div[@id='ajaxdiv']")
```

3. Run your tests, as shown in the following screenshot:

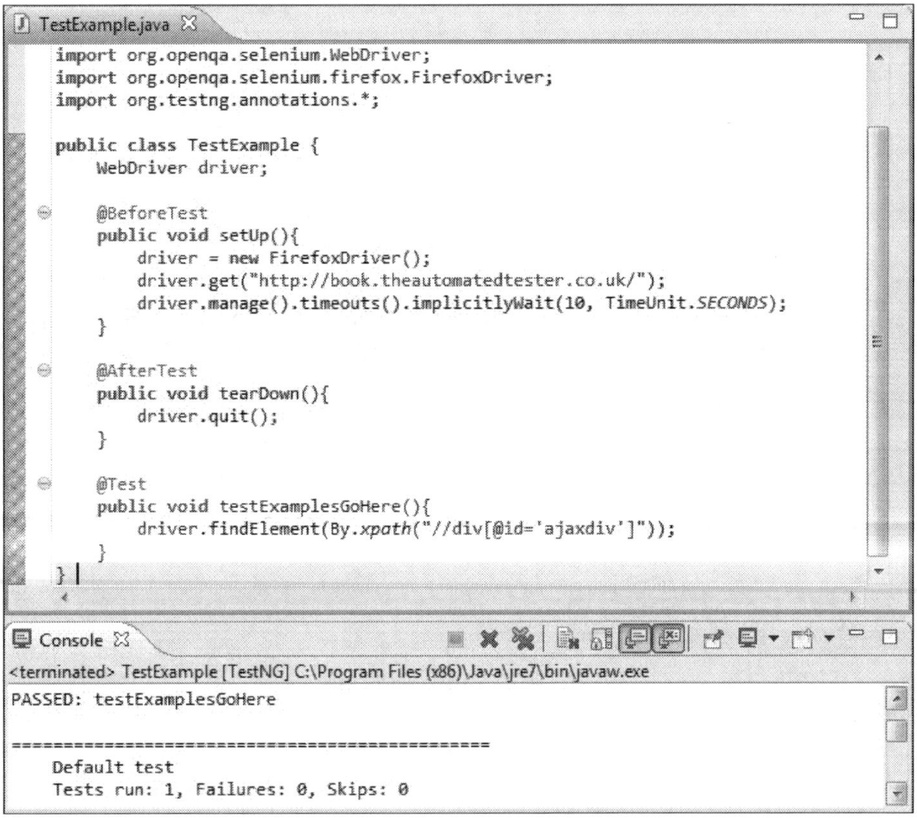

```
TestExample.java ⊠
    import org.openqa.selenium.WebDriver;
    import org.openqa.selenium.firefox.FirefoxDriver;
    import org.testng.annotations.*;

    public class TestExample {
        WebDriver driver;

        @BeforeTest
        public void setUp(){
            driver = new FirefoxDriver();
            driver.get("http://book.theautomatedtester.co.uk/");
            driver.manage().timeouts().implicitlyWait(10, TimeUnit.SECONDS);
        }

        @AfterTest
        public void tearDown(){
            driver.quit();
        }

        @Test
        public void testExamplesGoHere(){
            driver.findElement(By.xpath("//div[@id='ajaxdiv']"));
        }
    }
```

```
Console ⊠
<terminated> TestExample [TestNG] C:\Program Files (x86)\Java\jre7\bin\javaw.exe
PASSED: testExamplesGoHere

===============================================
    Default test
    Tests run: 1, Failures: 0, Skips: 0
```

We have just seen our test run and pass. We didn't have to do anything special to wait for the new text to appear on the page. Let's see how we can do this with the explicit waiting approach.

Explicit waits

Unfortunately, implicit waits do not fit all situations. For some developers, this is not the right thing to do. We use explicit waits when we know what we want to happen and the error needs to fit this situation.

Let's see this in action!

Using explicit waits with Selenium WebDriver

In this section, we will take a look at how to use explicit waits. This is useful to make sure that the right type of exception is thrown:

1. Open your Java IDE.

2. Use the following code. The `WebDriverWait` class is found in the support package within the Selenium WebDriver JAR:

```
WebElement element = (new WebDriverWait(driver, 10))
  .until(new ExpectedCondition<WebElement>(){
    @Override
    public WebElement apply(WebDriver d) {
      return d.findElement(By.xpath("//div[@id='ajaxdiv']"));
}});
```

3. Run your tests, as shown in the following screenshot:

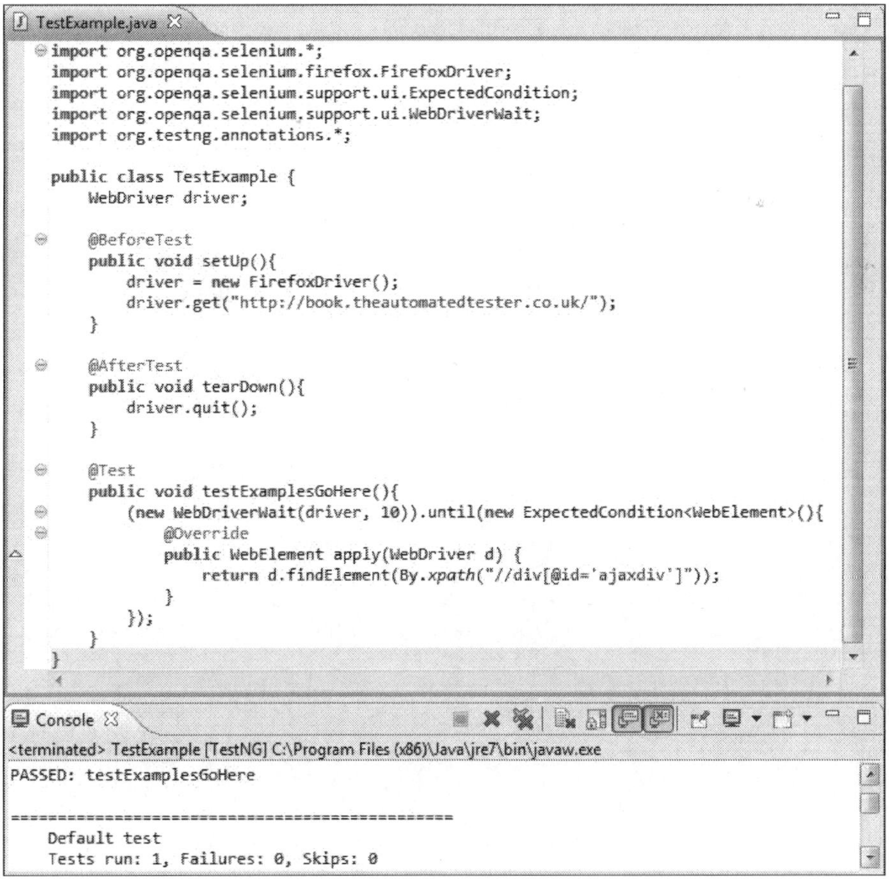

We have just seen how we can use an explicit wait with our code. We told the wait class that we wanted it to wait ten seconds while trying to find the element. I personally prefer explicit waits, as you can see by reading the code how long it is going to wait for.

Let's now see what we have learned in this chapter.

Summary

In this chapter, you learned how to find elements using Selenium WebDriver elements.

Specifically, we covered:

- **Finding elements with helper methods**: We saw what is needed to get things running and how to find elements on the page using Selenium WebDriver. We started with the helper methods to just start finding elements. In the following section, we saw how we can make them more robust.

- **Finding elements in a maintainable way**: In this section, we learned how to find elements with a more maintainable approach. We just had to change the argument in the method signature.

- **Tips and tricks**: Here, we learned how to find an element without throwing an exception. We also looked at waiting for elements to appear on the page. Elements can happen asynchronously, so we never know when they will appear.

- **List Of locating elements using WebDriver**: WebDriver locatea elements on the page using the By abstract class. In WebDriver automation everything is related to web elements. WebElement is a DOM object appearing on the web page:

  ```
  Java syntax: WebElement element = driver.
  findElement(By.<Locator>);
  ```

In the preceding statement, you have to specify the locator to identify the web element. In the By class, we have different static methods to identify elements.

The following are the locators listed in the table with examples used in WebDriver:

Locators	Example
`By.id`	`WebElement element = driver.findElement(By.id("inputButton"))`
`By.name`	`WebElement element = driver.findElement(By.name("buttonName"))`
`By.className`	`WebElement element = driver.findElement(By.className("name"))`
`By.cssSelector`	`WebElement element = driver.findElement(By.cssSelector("#inputButton"))`
`By.linkText`	`WebElement element = driver.findElement(By.linkText("click here"))`
`By.partialLinkText`	`WebElement element = driver.findElement(By.partialLinkText("here"))`
`By.tagName`	`WebElement element = driver.findElement(By.tagName("span"))`
`By.xpath`	`WebElement element = driver.findElement(By.xpath("//button[@id='btn']"))`

Now that we've learned about finding elements, we're ready to start using browsers and tweaking them to our needs, which is the topic of the next chapter.

Self-test questions

1. What is the best call to find multiple elements using XPath?

    a. `findElementByXpath`

    b. `findElementsByXPath`

    c. `findElementByCssSelector`

2. What is the best call to an element using CSS selectors to find an element by using only the class name?

    a. `findElementById`

    b. `findElementsByCssSelector`

    c. `findElementByClassName`

3. Will a `findElements` type call throw a `NoSuchElementException` when it can't find the element?

4. What is the difference between an explicit wait and an implicit wait?

5
Design Patterns

A design pattern is a general reusable solution to a commonly occurring problem within a given context in software design. In this chapter, we will take a look at good design patterns to create maintainable and reusable bits of code that we can use with our Selenium tests. This means that, if there are any changes needed to our web application, or any changes in the way we need to find elements, we can change them once and have things fixed very quickly.

In this chapter, we will learn the following topics:

- Using Page Object design
- Using the `PageFactory` Selenium library in Page objects
- Using the `LoadableComponents` Selenium library

In this chapter, it is assumed that all files will have the following `import` statements:

```
import org.openqa.selenium.By;
import org.openqa.selenium.WebDriver;
import org.openqa.selenium.WebElement;
import org.openqa.selenium.support.FindBy;
```

So let's get on with it.

Page objects

In this section of the chapter, we will take a look at how we can apply some best code practices to tests. You will learn how to make maintainable test suites that allow you to update tests in seconds. We will also take a look at how to create your own DSL (**Domain-specific language**) so that people can see intent. Also, we will create tests using the Page Object pattern.

Let's start trying to put these best practices to work.

Setting up the test

Imagine that you have a number of tests that work on a site that requires you to log in and move to a certain page. Or, imagine that you need to have a test that requires you to be on a certain page. In these two situations, the quickest way to find out which page you are on and then move to the correct one if need be, is to start testing. This is to make sure that we follow one of the major tenants of test automation. In this, you always start from a known place. Let's see this in an example:

1. Create a new Java class in Eclipse IDE.

2. Import the relevant Selenium packages.

3. Create the `setup()` and `teardown()` methods. I prefer the JUnit 4 style of tests and show code samples with the annotations.

4. We need to verify that the page object is on the correct page. For this, we will use `selenium.getTitle` to see the page title. If it is incorrect, move to `http://book.theautomatedtester.co.uk/chapter2`. We do this as navigating to the page is slower than checking the page's title or any other calls to the page already loaded.

5. We need to then verify that it is correct and work accordingly. The following is a code snippet of how we can do this:

```
if (!"Page 2".equals(selenium.getTitle())){
   selenium.get(
     "http://book.theautomatedtester.co.uk/chapter2");
}
```

6. Create the rest of the test to verify that items are on the page.

We have just seen how we can check whether something is what the test is expecting. If it is, the test will carry on as usual. If it isn't what we expect, we can move our test to the correct page and then carry on with this page. We will verify that if you log into `@Before`, you might not start your tests.

Now, let's take a look at how we can make more tests maintainable by splitting areas out into other methods.

Moving Selenium steps into private methods to make tests maintainable

Imagine that you just need to test one page on your site and you have quite a few tests for this page. A lot of the tests will be using the same code over and over again.

This can be quite annoying to maintain. If something changes on the page, we will have to go through all the tests to fix this one issue.

The way to fix this is to refactor the tests so that they are simpler and easier to read. Let's create a number of tests like the following:

```
@Test
public void shouldCheckButtonOnChapter2Page(){
   selenium.get("http://book.theautomatedtester.co.uk");
   selenium.findElement(By.linkText("Chapter2")).click();
   Assert.assertEquals
     (selenium.findElements(By.id("but1")).size(), 1);
}

@Test
public void shouldCheckAnotherButtonOnChapter2Page(){
   selenium.get("http://book.theautomatedtester.co.uk");
   selenium.findElement(By.linkText("Chapter2")).click();
   Assert.assertEquals
     (selenium.findElements(By.id("verifybutton")).size(), 1);
}
```

Using the previous examples, let's break these tests down:

1. In both the examples, we can see that they open the root of the website. Let's move this into its own private method. To do this in Eclipse IDE, you highlight the lines you want to refactor and then right-click. Use the context menu for **Refactor** and then click on **Extract Method**:

Refactor	Alt+Shift+T ▸	Move...	Alt+Shift+V
Surround With	Alt+Shift+Z ▸	Change Method Signature...	Alt+Shift+C
Local History	▸	Extract Method...	Alt+Shift+M
References	▸	Extract Local Variable...	Alt+Shift+L
Declarations	▸	Inline...	Alt+Shift+I
Run As	▸	Extract Interface...	
Debug As	▸	Extract Superclass...	
Apply Checkstyle fixes	Ctrl+Alt+C	Use Supertype Where Possible...	
Team	▸	Pull Up...	
Compare With	▸	Push Down...	
Replace With	▸	Extract Class...	
Checkstyle	▸	Introduce Parameter Object...	

2. Then you will see a dialog box asking you to give a name to the method. Provide a meaningful name for the method. I have called it `loadHomePage`, as you can see in the following screenshot:

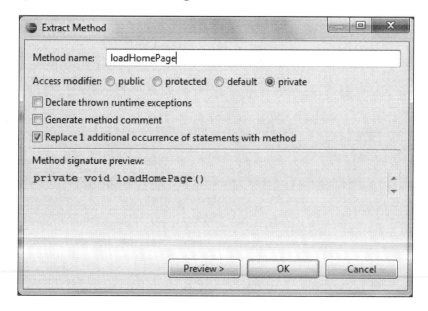

3. Now, do the same for the other parts of the tests so that it makes the test look a lot more succinct.

4. Your test class should look something like the following code:

```
@Test
public void shouldCheckButtonOnChapter2Page(){
  loadHomePage();
  clickAndLoadChapter2();
  Assert.assertEquals(selenium.findElements(
    By.id("but1")).size(), 1);
}

@Test
public void shouldCheckAnotherButtonOnChapter2Page(){
  loadHomePage();
  clickAndLoadChapter2();
  Assert.assertEquals(selenium.findElements(
    By.id("verifybutton")).size(), 1);
}
```

```
private void loadHomePage() {
    selenium.get("http://book.theautomatedtester.co.uk");
}

private void clickAndLoadChapter2() {
    selenium.findElement(By.linkText("Chapter2")).click();
}
```

We have just started making our tests a lot more maintainable. We saw how we can break this down into more succinct and readable tests that show intent, rather than showing a test as a clump of Selenium calls. This also makes the tests a lot more manageable because, if we were to change the link on the root from Chapter2 to Chapter 2, I would only need to fix it in one place rather than *n* places, where *n* is the number of times that sequence is in the test class.

Now, let's take a look at how we can use the Page Object pattern for creating a DSL over the site.

Using the Page Object pattern to design tests

Imagine that you have a site that has a number of different pages that you need to test. This is quite common for a number of sites. We can create an object that represents the page and then pass the Selenium object as a parameter. So, let's now create our first Page Object against the home page:

1. Create a new Java class in Eclipse IDE called HomePage.
2. Import the relevant packages for the tests to run.

We will now need a constructor to handle Selenium. You might want to make it go to the home page when it's instantiated too. An example of this can be seen in the following code snippets:

- HomePage.java

```
import org.openqa.selenium.By;
import org.openqa.selenium.WebDriver;

public class HomePage{
    WebDriver selenium;
    public HomePage(WebDriver selenium){
        this.selenium = selenium;
    }
    public Chapter2 clickChapter2(){
        clickChapter("2");
```

```
      return new Chapter2(selenium);
    }

    private void clickChapter(String number){
      selenium.findElement(By.linkText("Chapter"+number)).click();
    }
}
```

- Chapter2.java

```
import org.openqa.selenium.By;
import org.openqa.selenium.WebDriver;

public class Chapter2 {
  WebDriver selenium;
  public Chapter2(WebDriver selenium){
    this.selenium = selenium;
    if (!"Chapter 2".equalsIgnoreCase(
      this.selenium.getTitle())){
        selenium.get(
          "http://book.theautomatedtester.co.uk/chapter2");
      }
  }
  public boolean isButtonPresent(String button){
    return selenium.findElements(By.xpath("//input[@id='" +
      button + "']")).size()>0;
  }
}
```

- BestPractises3.java

```
import org.junit.After;
import org.junit.Before;
import org.junit.Test;
import org.openqa.selenium.WebDriver;
import org.openqa.selenium.firefox.FirefoxDriver;

public class BestPractises3 {
  WebDriver selenium;

  @Before
  public void setUp(){
    selenium = new FirefoxDriver();
  }
```

```
    @After
    public void tearDown(){
        selenium.quit();
    }

    @Test
    public void
        ShouldLoadTheHomePageAndThenCheckButtonOnChapter2(){
        selenium.get("http://book.theautomatedtester.co.uk");
        HomePage hp = new HomePage(selenium);
        Chapter2 ch2 = hp.clickChapter2();
        assertTrue(ch2.isButtonPresent("but1"));
    }
}
```

If you create these three files, you will see it pass. The test is a lot more succinct and easier to maintain.

In this section, we had a look at how to create tests using the Page Object design pattern. This allows us to create objects in a programming language and then pass the Selenium object to it to drive the browser. This creates a really nice DSL that allows all parties in the development cycle to follow. We create a Java object for each of the pages that we want to work against on the site. We then just need to instantiate the class to work against this page.

When we are moving between pages, you can click on a link and the method controlling the page transition will return an object that represents a new page.

The objects will not hold the asserts; this should always be done within the tests.

Using Page Factory with Page Object

The code that we learned to write earlier can be quite verbose. To clean up our code, we can start to use Page Factories. This allows us to annotate variables in our page objects about how to search the page. It means that we don't need to have the complete `WebElement element = driver.findElement(...);` code all over the file. We can change it to:

```
@FindBy(how=How.ID, using="foo")
WebElement foo;
```

As you can see, this can make our code slightly easier to read and more maintainable. If you regularly use other languages (such as Ruby or Python), you will notice that they don't have the `PageFactory` support project. This is because these languages don't have `Factory` constructs in the language. They are not idiomatic and therefore not in the language.

To use the `PageFactory` project in WebDriver, we will have to ensure its addition as a dependency.

Let's now update our previous code with an example of the `PageFactory` project.

Using PageFactory

In this example, we will clean up the previous examples using `PageFactory`. This allows us to create more succinct code compared to the previous verbose examples.

Open the previous example and go to `Chapter2.java`. It should look like the following example:

- `Chapter2.java`:

```java
import org.openqa.selenium;
import junit.framework.Assert;

public class Chapter2 {
  WebDriver selenium;
  WebElement verifybutton;

  public Chapter2(WebDriver selenium){
    this.selenium = selenium;
    verifybutton = selenium.findElement(By.id("verifybutton"));
    if (!"Chapter 2".equalsIgnoreCase(
      this.selenium.getTitle())){
        selenium.get(
          "http://book.theautomatedtester.co.uk/chapter2");
      }
  }

  public boolean isButtonPresent(String button){
    return selenium.findElements(By.xpath
      ("//input[@id='"+button+"']")).size()>0;
  }

}
```

We can then change the line that looks for `verifybutton` so that it is not in the constructor. This changes to:

```
public class Chapter2 {
  WebDriver selenium;

  @FindBy(how= How.NAME, using="verifybutton")
  WebElement verifybutton;

  public Chapter2(WebDriver selenium){
    this.selenium = selenium;
    if (!"Chapter 2".equalsIgnoreCase(
      this.selenium.getTitle())){
        selenium.get(
          "http://book.theautomatedtester.co.uk/chapter2");
      }
  }

  public boolean isButtonPresent(String button){
    return selenium.findElements(By.xpath
    ("//input[@id='"+button+"']")).size()>0;
  }

}
```

If you run your test now, you will see it perform the same action, but we have not called the `findElement()` method that is available to WebDriver.

In the test, we need to initialize the factory by calling `initElements()`:

- `TestChapter2.java`:

```
import org.openqa.selenium.*;
import org.junit.*;

public class TestChapter2 {
  WebDriver selenium;

  @Before
  public void setUp(){
    selenium = new FirefoxDriver();
  }

  @After
  public void tearDown(){
```

```
        selenium.quit();
    }

    public Chapter2 clickChapter2(){
        clickChapter("2");
        return   PageFactory.initElements(selenium, Chapter2.class);
    }
    @Test
    public void ShouldLoadTheHomePageAndThenCheckButtonOnChapter2()
    {
        selenium.get("http://book.theautomatedtester.co.uk");
        HomePage hp = new HomePage(selenium);
        Chapter2 ch2 = hp.clickChapter2();
        assertTrue(ch2.isButtonPresent("but1"));
    }


}
```

We have just seen how we can get rid of a line of code from a constructor or a method by adding a decorator to the variable. When our code is compiled, the variable will get populated at the right time so that we can make sure that it gets the right bit of the DOM. It will look like our element hasn't been instantiated. When we initialize `PageFactory`, by calling `initElements()`, it will populate the variables with the right data.

This does make a lot of the code a lot more concise and can be a lot easier to maintain over time.

One thing to note here is that every time we use the element it will be searched. We can get Selenium WebDriver to cache the return of the results by adding another decorator:

```
@FindBy(how=How.ID, using="verifybutton")
@CacheLookup
WebElement verifybutton;
```

> We only want to cache the result on a fairly static page. If you have a site that has a lot of JavaScript, you will not want to use @CacheLookup as you might start getting StaleElementException when you try it.

LoadableComponent

LoadableComponent is another way to approach Page Objects. LoadableComponent is a base class that all of the pages need to extend. The base class has the following methods on the interface:

- get()
- isLoaded()
- load()

Instead of the usual public class PageObject, we change it to:

```
public class PageObject extends LoadableComponent<PageObject>
```

We will have to add overrides for the load() and isLoaded() method. The load() method loads the page for us and the isLoaded() method allows us to check whether the page has been loaded correctly.

For example, check the following piece of code:

```
@override
Protected void load() {
  selenium.get("http://book.theautomatedtester.co.uk");
}

@protected void isLoaded() {
  String url = selenium.getCurrentUrl();
  If (url != "http://book.theautomatedtester.co.uk"){
    throw new Exception("The wrong page has loaded");
  }
}
```

As we can see, this is just a simple bit of code, but we can make sure that we start on the right page when we need to.

Changing our Page Object to use LoadableComponent

Now that we have learned about LoadableComponents, we should have a look at it in action. We need to make changes to our Java class.

1. The following is how the code should look so far:

```
public class Chapter2 {
  WebDriver selenium;
```

```
@FindBy(how= How.NAME, using="verifybutton")
WebElement verifybutton;

public Chapter2(WebDriver selenium){
   this.selenium = selenium;
   if (!"Chapter 2".equalsIgnoreCase(this.selenium.getTitle())){
      selenium.get
         ("http://book.theautomatedtester.co.uk/chapter2");
   }
}

public boolean isButtonPresent(String button){
   return selenium.findElements
      (By.xpath("//input[@id='"+button+"']")).size()>0;
   }
}
```

2. If we have a look at our `Chapter2` Java class, we can see that we need to extend `LoadableComponent`. As this takes generics, we will have to pass it in our `PageObject` class. It should look like the following line of code:

```
public class Chapter2 extends LoadableComponent<Chapter2> {
```

3. In our constructor, we will have to initialize our Page Factory. We can remove the rest of the code in here as this will be moved to `load()`. It should look like the following code snippet:

```
public Chapter2(WebDriver selenium){
   this.selenium = selenium;
   PageFactory.initElements(selenium, this);
}
```

4. We now need to add our override methods. These allow us to check whether we are on the right page when we load this component:

```
@override
Protected void load() {
   selenium.get("http://book.theautomatedtester.co.uk/chapter2");
}

@protected void isLoaded() {
   String url = selenium.getCurrentUrl();
   If (url != "http://book.theautomatedtester.co.uk/chapter2"){
      throw new Exception("The wrong page has loaded");
   }
}
```

5. Now we need to update our test to load everything for us. To do this, we need to change as follows:

```
@Test
public void ShouldLoadTheHomePageAndThenCheckButtonOnChapter2() {
    selenium.get("http://book.theautomatedtester.co.uk");
    HomePage hp = new HomePage(selenium);
    Chapter2 ch2 = hp.clickChapter2();
    assertTrue(ch2.isButtonPresent("but1"));
}
```

6. It should then look like this:

```
@Test
public void ShouldLoadTheHomePageAndThenCheckButtonOnChapter2(){
    Chapter2 cht = new Chapter2(selenium).get();

    cht. isButtonDisplayed ("but1");
}
```

7. Run your test. Everything should look like the following code snippet:

```
public class Chapter2 extends LoadableComponent<Chapter2>{
    WebDriver selenium;

    @FindBy(how= How.NAME, using="verifybutton")
    WebElement verifybutton;

    public Chapter2(WebDriver selenium){
        this.selenium = selenium;
        PageFactory.initElements(selenium, this);
    }

    @Override
    Protected void load() {
        selenium.get("http://book.theautomatedtester.co.uk/chapter2");
    }

    @Override
    protected void isLoaded() {
        String url = selenium.getCurrentUrl();
        If (url != "http://book.theautomatedtester.co.uk/chapter2"){
            throw new Exception("The wrong page has loaded");
        }
    }
```

```
        public boolean isButtonDisplayed(String button){
          return selenium.findElement(By.id("button")).isDisplayed();
        }
    }
```

We have just converted our page object to use the LoadableComponent class that comes with the Selenium project. We saw how we simplified constructors and then just moved this into somewhere easy to maintain. We also saw that we can move a lot of the boiler plate code out of our class and rely on it being pulled in via LoadableComponent. This means that we no longer need to maintain it, or we add these items.

Using LoadableComponent

Imagine that you have to work with a flow that takes you through a number of pages. LoadableComponent allows us to set up a workflow. To get this right, we need to pass in something like the following code snippet while performing your test setup:

```
@Before
public void prepareComponents() {
    WebDriver selenium = new FirefoxDriver();

    HomePage homePage = new HomePage(selenium);
    Chapter2 chapter2 = new SecuredPage(selenium, homePage);

}
```

Summary

In this chapter, we learned about design patterns that we can use with Selenium WebDriver. We learned techniques that allow us to build test projects that are easy to maintain and readable by all users.

Specifically, we covered:

- **Page Objects**: This is a technique where we split the test logic into separate classes. This allows us to create a Java class for each of the pages that we use on the page.

- **Page Factory**: This allows us to decorate our WebElement variables in our Page objects so that we remove a lot of the look up code. We learned that the elements get initialized when we call PageFactory.initElements(); in our tests or anything else that might use this code.

- `LoadableComponent`: In this section, we had a look at the base page for Page Objects that comes with the Selenium project. The `LoadableComponent` in a base class that allows us to remove quite a bit of code and moves the boilerplate to `LoadableComponent`.

Now that we've learned about design patterns, we're ready to look at the last advanced techniques that we can use with Selenium WebDriver, which is the topic of the next chapter.

Self-test questions

1. What is Page Object design pattern?
2. What is the decorator that you put above a `WebElement` variable while looking for an element by ID with `id='myId'`?
3. How do you cache the lookup of web elements?
4. How do you initialize a Page Factory?

6
Working with WebDriver

In *Chapter 4, Finding Elements*, we saw how we can look for elements. Now let's start working with Selenium WebDriver in different browsers. Remember that Selenium WebDriver is a browser automation framework for all of the major browsers and can access a browser like an end user would.

In this chapter, we will:

- Run a test with Firefox and work with Firefox profiles
- Run a test with Google Chrome or Chromium
- Update the capabilities of the browser
- Run a test with Opera and work with Opera profiles
- Run a test with Internet Explorer
- Work with `InternetExplorerDriver`

So, let's get on with it.

You will need to download the following items. Make sure that you download the relevant executable for your environment:

- **IE Driver Executable**: This can be downloaded from `http://code.google.com/p/selenium/downloads/list`
- **Chrome Driver Executable**: This can be downloaded from `http://code.google.com/p/chromium/downloads/list`
- **Opera Driver Executable**: This can be downloaded from `https://github.com/operasoftware/operadriver/downloads`
- Firefox Driver does not require a download as it is bundled with the Java client bindings.

Please make sure that you have all the necessary browsers installed to complete all the sections of this chapter.

When working through the following examples, we will assume that you have instantiated a WebDriver object by typing the following line of code:

```
WebDriver driver = new FirefoxDriver();
```

You can use the following example class with TestNG:

```
import org.openqa.selenium.WebDriver;
import org.openqa.selenium.firefox.FirefoxDriver;
import org.testng.annotations.AfterTest;
import org.testng.annotations.BeforeTest;
import org.testng.annotations.Test;

public class TestChapter6 {

  WebDriver driver;

  @BeforeTest
  public void setUp(){
    driver = //we will update this part with each section
    driver.get("http://book.theautomatedtester.co.uk/chapter4");
    }

  @AfterTest
  public void tearDown(){
    driver.quit();
  }

  @Test
  public void testExamples(){
    // We will put examples in here
  }
}
```

Working with FirefoxDriver

Everything we need to use in FirefoxDriver is bundled with the Java client bindings, which we used in *Chapter 5, Design Patterns*. This makes the driver easy to use.

We will do the basic task of loading the browser and type the following into the page:

1. Update the `setUp()` method to load `FirefoxDriver();`.

   ```
   driver = new FirefoxDriver();
   ```

2. Now we need to find an element. In this section, we will find the one with the `nextBid` ID:

   ```
   WebElement element = driver.findElement(By.id("nextBid"));
   ```

3. Now we need to type the following line of code into that element:

   ```
   element.sendKeys("100");
   ```

4. Run your test and it should look like the following:

   ```
   import org.openqa.selenium.*;
   import org.openqa.selenium.firefox.*;
   import org.testng.annotations.*;

   public class TestChapter6 {

     WebDriver driver;

     @BeforeTest
     public void setUp(){
       driver = new FirefoxDriver();
       driver.get("http://book.theautomatedtester.co.uk/chapter4");
     }

     @AfterTest
     public void tearDown(){
       driver.quit();
     }

     @Test
     public void testExamples(){
       WebElement element = driver.findElement(By.id("nextBid"));
       element.sendKeys("100");
     }
   }
   ```

We just saw how easy it is to run a test with Selenium WebDriver and Firefox. It loaded the browser and then typed the command into the browser. We can now do everything and anything that we want to the content that is loaded into the browser. Now let's have a look at all the other things that we can do with FirefoxDriver.

Firefox profile preferences

There are times when we need to update preferences within Firefox. This can be to switch on parts of Firefox that are disabled while they are in development, or if you want to get more information from the browser while your tests are running. To do this, we need to instantiate a Firefox profile object and then update the settings.

We then need to pass this object into FirefoxDriver, where we will instantiate it. This will load the profile with the details you have set. This is like loading about:config in the browser and changing what you need to.

Let's see how we can set Firefox preferences with a sample code. Imagine that you wanted to have your site as the startup page for Firefox. To do this, we need to update the browser.startup.homepage preference. Follow these steps:

1. Let's start by creating the FirefoxProfile object:

    ```
    FirefoxProfile profile = new FirefoxProfile();
    ```

2. Now, we will set the preference:

    ```
    profile.setPreference("browser.startup.homepage",
        "http://book.theautomatedtester.co.uk");
    ```

3. To get the profile to be used, we need to pass it into the driver. To do this, we need to do the following:

    ```
    driver = new FirefoxDriver(profile);
    ```

4. Run your test. The final code should look like the following:

    ```
    import org.openqa.selenium.*;
    import org.openqa.selenium.firefox.*;
    import org.testng.annotations.*;
    public class TestChapter6 {

        WebDriver driver;

        @BeforeTest
        public void setUp(){
        FirefoxProfile profile = new FirefoxProfile();
        profile.setPreference("browser.startup.homepage",
          "http://book.theautomatedtester.co.uk/chapter4");
          driver = new FirefoxDriver(profile);
          }
    ```

```
@AfterTest
public void tearDown(){
  driver.quit();
}

@Test
public void testExamples(){
  WebElement element = driver.findElement(By.id("nextBid"));
  element.sendKeys("100");
}
}
```

We just saw that we can manipulate Firefox settings before the browser is loaded. This is useful if you need to get extra information out of the browser or if you have a few things that need tweaking.

If you installed Firefox in a different place, you will have had to instantiate the `FirefoxBinary` class with details of it:

```
FirefoxBinary binary = new FirefoxBinary("/path/to/binary");
driver = new FirefoxDriver(binary);
```

If you need to update both the Firefox profile and the Firefox binary, you can simply pass both of them through the constructor as follows:

```
FirefoxBinary binary = new FirefoxBinary("/path/to/binary");
FirefoxProfile profile = new FirefoxProfile();
profile.setPreference("browser.startup.homepage",
  "http://book.theautomatedtester.co.uk/chapter4");

driver = new FirefoxDriver(binary, profile);
```

As you can see, it's fairly simple to load Firefox if it isn't installed in the usual place.

Installing a Firefox add-on

One of the most useful features of Firefox is the ability to install add-ons to enhance the user experience. This enhanced experience can mean that web applications act differently when the add-on is installed.

Let's have a look at how we can install an add-on into our profile before we open the browser.

Imagine that you wanted to install Firebug so that, if a test were to fail, we can try and debug JavaScript. To do this, we need to create a `FirefoxProfile` object and then tell it to add the add-on:

1. Create a profile object:

```
FirefoxProfile profile = new FirefoxProfile();
```

2. Now we need to install the add-on. WebDriver can only install add-ons that are on the local hard drive:

```
profile.addExtension("path/to/addon");
```

3. Pass the profile into FirefoxDriver and then run your test. Your code will look like the following:

```
import org.openqa.selenium.*;
import org.openqa.selenium.firefox.*;
 import org.testng.annotations.*;
public class TestChapter6 {

    WebDriver driver;

    @BeforeTest
    public void setUp(){
        FirefoxProfile profile = new FirefoxProfile();
        profile.addExtension("firebug.xpi");
        driver = new FirefoxDriver(profile);
        driver.get("http://book.theautomatedtester.co.uk/chapter4");
    }

    @AfterTest
    public void tearDown(){
        driver.quit();
    }

    @Test
    public void testExamples(){
        WebElement element = driver.findElement(By.id("nextBid"));
        element.sendKeys("100");
    }
}
```

We have just installed a Firefox add-on into the browser before we run our test. This is much simpler than it used to be in Selenium Remote Control, where we will need to load the profile manually and make the changes that we needed and then run our tests telling the Selenium server to use this profile. The old process is not very portable compared to what we just did.

So far, we learned to load Firefox and make changes to the browser before it loads, which is quite useful if we need to get more information out of the browser or make debugging issues a lot simpler.

A lot of people like to use Firebug with WebDriver but get really annoyed with the first run page.

1. To get around this, we have to update the version of Firebug in our Firefox preferences.

2. We will set the version to 99.9:

```java
import java.io.File;
import org.openqa.selenium.*;
import org.openqa.selenium.firefox.*;
import org.testng.annotations.*;

public class TestChapter6 {

    WebDriver driver;

    @BeforeTest
    public void setUp(){
        FirefoxProfile profile = new FirefoxProfile();
        profile.addExtension("firebug.xpi");
        profile.setPreference
            ("extensions.firebug.currentVersion", "99.9");
        driver = new FirefoxDriver(profile);
        driver.get
            ("http://book.theautomatedtester.co.uk/chapter4");
    }

    @AfterTest
    public void tearDown(){
        driver.quit();
    }

    @Test
    public void testExamples(){
        WebElement element =
            driver.findElement(By.id("nextBid"));
        element.sendKeys("100");
    }
}
```

Working with ChromeDriver

In this section, we will have a look at how we can start working with Google Chrome or with Chromium. Google Chrome or Chromium is in the top three browsers used in the world, so most people want to make sure that their web applications work with it.

If you haven't downloaded ChromeDriver, you will need to do it now for the following sections. You will also need to set an environment path to where it is, so ChromeDriver in Java will know where to get it. This is purely for ChromeDriver. If you have Google Chrome or Chromium installed somewhere that isn't the default, we will see how to handle that with ChromeOptions.

On Linux and Mac OS X, `export PATH=$PATH:/path/to/chromedriver`.

On Windows, set `PATH=$PATH;\path\to\chromedriver`.

Imagine that you wanted to work with Google Chrome to get an attribute of an element on the page. To do this, we will need to instantiate ChromeDriver. Let's see an example:

1. Update the `setUp()` method to load `ChromeDriver()`:

   ```
   driver = new ChromeDriver();
   ```

2. Now we will need to find an element. In this section, we will find the one with the `selectLoad` ID:

   ```
   WebElement element = driver.findElement(By.id("selectLoad"));
   ```

3. Now, we will need to get the value attribute of the previous element:

   ```
   element.getAttribute("value");
   ```

4. Run your test and it should look like the following:

   ```
   import org.openqa.selenium.*;
   import org.openqa.selenium.chrome.ChromeDriver;
   import org.testng.Assert;
   import org.testng.annotations.*;

   public class TestChapter6 {

       WebDriver driver;

       @BeforeTest
       public void setUp(){
   ```

```
    driver = new ChromeDriver();
    driver.get("http://book.theautomatedtester.co.uk/chapter4");
}


@AfterTest
public void tearDown(){
  driver.quit();
}


@Test
public void testExamples(){
  WebElement element = driver.findElement(
    By.id("selectLoad"));
  String value = element.getAttribute("value");
  Assert.assertEquals("Click to load the select below",
    value);
  }
}
```

We just ran a test with Google Chrome or with Chromium. It was fairly simple to get going and then the browser was able to get the value of the button. If you had trouble getting it to run, make sure that you have downloaded ChromeDriver and added it to the environment variable called PATH.

Now that we have got ChromeDriver working, let's have a look at how we can update the browser as we did with Firefox.

ChromeOptions

Google Chrome or Chromium doesn't really have a profile that users can update in the same sense as Firefox. It does, however, have a mechanism that allows us to set certain options that Chrome will try and use. We can also tell it to install Chromium extensions, which are like Firefox add-ons, into the browser so that we can enhance the experience.

Imagine that you needed to tell ChromeDriver the location of your Google Chrome or Chromium. To set this, we will need to instantiate a ChromeOptions object and tell it where to find the Chrome/Chromium binary.

Let's see how to do it:

1. Update the `setUp()` method to instantiate a `ChromeOptions` object and call the `setBinary()` method:

   ```
   ChromeOptions options = new ChromeOptions();
   options.setBinary("/path/to/location");
   ```

2. Update the `setUp()` method to load the `ChromeOptions` object into ChromeDriver:

   ```
   driver = new ChromeDriver(options);
   ```

3. Now we will need to find an element. In this section, we will find the one with the `selectLoad` ID:

   ```
   WebElement element = driver.findElement(By.id("selectLoad"));
   ```

4. Now we will need to get the value attribute of that element:

   ```
   element.getAttribute("value");
   ```

5. Run your test and it should look like the following:

   ```java
   import org.openqa.selenium.*;
   import org.openqa.selenium.chrome.ChromeDriver;
   import org.testng.Assert;
   import org.testng.annotations.*;

   public class TestChapter6 {

     WebDriver driver;

     @BeforeTest
     public void setUp(){
       ChromeOptions options = new ChromeOptions();
       options.setBinary("/path/to/location");
       driver = new ChromeDriver(options);
       driver.get("http://book.theautomatedtester.co.uk/chapter4");
     }

     @AfterTest
     public void tearDown(){
       driver.quit();
     }

     @Test
     public void testExamples(){
   ```

```
WebElement element = driver.findElement(
By.id("selectLoad"));
String value = element.getAttribute("value");
Assert.assertEquals("Click to load the select below",
  value);
    }
}
```

We just saw how we can inject the options that we want, Chrome or Chromium to start with. If we need to pass in the arguments that we want to start the browser with or if we need to tell ChromeDriver, we can use `setArguments()`. This allows us to do many things to the browser. We can see a definitive list at `http://src.chromium.org/viewvc/chrome/trunk/src/chrome/common/chrome_switches.cc?view=markup`.

If you have a Chrome extension, a file with a `.crx` extension, you will need to use the `addExtension()` method as you would in FirefoxDriver. The following snippet will show an example:

```
ChromeOptions options = new ChromeOptions();
options.addExtension("example.crx")
```

Working with OperaDriver

Opera Software, the company that created Opera, has built their own project to support Selenium WebDriver. Since not every web browser will act the same with the sites that we create, it is a good idea to make sure we can test our applications with OperaDriver.

 Note that OperaDriver works best with the latest stable release of Opera. Make sure that you update it regularly.

Let's see how easy OperaDriver is to use. In this section, we will see how we can start OperaDriver and get it to click a button on the page. This simple test will give us the confidence to use Selenium WebDriver with Opera:

1. Update the `setUp()` method to load `OperaDriver()`:

    ```
    driver = new OperaDriver();
    ```

2. Now we will need to find an element. In this section, we will find the link Chapter 4:

    ```
    WebElement element = driver.findElement(By.linkText("Chapter 4"));
    ```

3. Now we will need to click on the link:

```
element.click();
```

4. Run your test and it should look like the following:

```java
import org.openqa.selenium.*;
import org.testng.Assert;
import org.testng.annotations.*;
import com.opera.core.systems.OperaDriver;


public class TestChapter6 {

  WebDriver driver;

  @BeforeTest
  public void setUp(){
    driver = new OperaDriver();
    driver.get("http://book.theautomatedtester.co.uk/");
  }



  @AfterTest
  public void tearDown(){
    driver.quit();
  }

  @Test
  public void testExamples(){
    WebElement element = driver.findElement(
      By.linkText("Chapter 4"));
    element.click();

    // Assert that we only have 1 link
    Assert.assertEquals(1, driver.findElements(
      By.linkText("index")).size());
  }
}
```

We just saw how easy it is to get OperaDriver loading Opera and interacting with what is on the page. We used `click()` on a link in order to navigate between pages. Just by changing the object that is instantiated in the `setUp()` method, we got it to load.

Opera, like the previous browsers we used, allows us to set the preferences of the browser before the browser has started up. Let's have a look at how that works.

OperaProfile

OperaProfile is a new addition to OperaDriver. It allows us to set preferences in the browser when the browser starts. Opera Software tests the browser where it can so that we can set a lot of details. In the following example, we will disable geolocation from our tests.

Imagine that you want to test your web application that uses geolocation in a browser, when this particular browser cannot use geolocation. All location-based applications need to support this to protect against privacy on certain machines:

1. Update the `setUp()` method to load `OperaDriver()`:

    ```
    OperaProfile profile = new OperaProfile();
    profile.preferences().set("Geolocation",
      "Enable geolocation", false);
    driver = new OperaDriver(profile);
    ```

2. Now we will need to find an element. In this section, we will find the link for `Chapter 4`:

    ```
    WebElement element = driver.findElement(By.linkTexxt(
      "Chapter 4"));
    ```

3. Now we will need to click on the link:

    ```
    element.click();
    ```

4. Run your test and it should look like the following:

    ```
    import org.openqa.selenium.*;
    import org.testng.Assert;
    import org.testng.annotations.*;
    import com.opera.core.systems.*;

    public class TestChapter6 {

      WebDriver driver;

      @BeforeTest
      public void setUp(){
        OperaProfile profile = new OperaProfile();
        profile.preferences().set("Geolocation",
          "Enable geolocation", false);
        driver = new OperaDriver(profile);
        driver.get("http://book.theautomatedtester.co.uk/");
    ```

```
    }

    @AfterTest
    public void tearDown(){
      driver.quit();
    }

    @Test
    public void testExamples(){
      WebElement element = driver.findElement(
        By.linkText("Chapter 4"));
      element.click();
      Assert.assertEquals(1, driver.findElements(
        By.linkText("index")).size());
    }
  }
```

We just saw how we can set a preference with Opera and then inject that into the browser so that, when the browser starts, it is there for us to use. As mentioned earlier, there are a lot of different preferences that can be set. To see a list of these, open Opera and use the URL, `http://www.opera.com/download/mirrors/config/` or visit `http://www.opera.com/support/usingopera/operaini/`.

Working with InternetExplorerDriver

Internet Explorer is the most commonly used browser in the world, followed by Firefox and Google Chrome, so getting IEDriver working is a high priority. The current version IEDriver supports IE6 through to IE9 so that you will be able to test websites that work on old browsers right up to the latest version of the browser.

If you haven't downloaded IEDriverServer, you will need to do it now for the following section. You will also need to set an environment path to where it is so that InternetExplorerDriver in Java will know where to get it. This is similar to what we did for the ChromeDriver earlier.

On Windows, set PATH=$PATH;\path\to\chromedriver.

In this section, we will get the text of the element on the page. This is something that most people have to do to check that the right things are happening on the page.

We will need to instantiate InternetExplorerDriver and the `getText()` call on the element. Let's get to it:

1. Update the `setUp()` method to load `InternetExplorerDriver()`:

```
driver = new InternetExplorerDriver();
```

2. Now we will need to find an element. In this section, we will find the link for Chapter 4:

```
WebElement element = driver.findElement(By.id("bid"));
```

3. Now we will need to get the text of the element:

```
element.getText();
```

4. Run your test and it should look like the following:

```java
import org.openqa.selenium.*;
import org.openqa.selenium.ie.InternetExplorerDriver;
import org.testng.Assert;
import org.testng.annotations.*;

public class TestChapter6 {

    WebDriver driver;

    @BeforeTest
    public void setUp(){
        driver = new InternetExplorerDriver();
        driver.get("http://book.theautomatedtester.co.uk/chapter4");

    }

    @AfterTest
    public void tearDown(){
     driver.quit();
    }

    @Test
    public void testExamples(){
        WebElement element = driver.findElement(By.id("bid"));
        Assert.assertEquals("50", element.getText());
    }
}
```

We just saw how we can use WebDriver to drive Internet Explorer. Since this is the most commonly used browser in the world, we always make sure that our applications work with it. As with all browsers, using Internet Explorer with WebDriver is really simple.

Other important points

You will notice that in the `tearDown()`, we call `quit()`. We call `quit()` because this call cleans up all of the resources that WebDriver starts up and uses. If you were to call `close()`, it will only close the window that Selenium WebDriver is currently on. On some implementations of the server-side, or browser code, when we use `close()` method and it is the last window open, then the server-side code will act as though `quit()` was called.

Summary

We learned a lot in this chapter about Selenium WebDriver and all of the different browsers that it supports and how we can use them.

Specifically, we covered the following topics:

- **FirefoxDriver**: We saw how easy it is to get started with WebDriver and Firefox and how we can go about setting preferences and installing add-ons. We also saw how we can tell FirefoxDriver where to launch Firefox from.

- **ChromeDriver**: This is another easy driver to use. Once we added the ChromeDriver executable that we downloaded to our PATH environment variable, we were able to use the driver. We also saw how we can tweak settings before the browser loads if we want to install extensions or if we want to set the location of the Chromium binary.

- **OperaDriver**: In this section, we learned how to use OperaDriver to work against our web application. We were also able to change the preferences of the browser before it loaded so that we can test it as users will find it.

- **InternetExplorerDriver**: In this section, we saw how we can use InternetExplorerDriver to drive Internet Explorer. We need to make sure that our applications work in Internet Explorer since it has the largest market share of any browser, so getting this right is essential.

We also discussed calling `quit()` when we are finished with WebDriver so that it can clean up resources.

Now that we've learned about desktop browsers, we're ready to learn about mobile browsers—which is the topic of the next chapter.

Self-test questions

1. How do you set a preference?

2. How do you tell FirefoxDriver to a version of Firefox that is not installed in the usual place?

3. What is the name of the object that allows us to tweak Chrome or Chromium before it launches?

4. What environment variable do we need to set and why?

5. Which version of the browser is recommended for use with OperaDriver?

6. How do we update browser preferences with OperaDriver?

7. Which versions of Internet Explorer does WebDriver support?

7
Automation Framework Development and Building Utilities

This chapter will be an introduction to automation framework, various types the automation frameworks, and the analysis of the best suitable automation framework for **AUT** (**Application Under Test**). You will learn the design and implementation of the *Keyword + Data driven = Hybrid* automation framework with the most successful methodology. We will also look into handling objects in practice, that is, using the Page Object factory concept using Selenium—WebDriver and TestNG on Eclipse.

Framework implementation contains integration of HTML reports and logs. This chapter will help you to build your own utilities for the framework.

In this chapter, you will learn about the following topics:

- Why use automation frameworks
- The evolution of frameworks and analysis
- Understanding **Hybrid Automation Framework** in detail, including architecture, design, and implementation using the Page Object factory concept using Selenium—Web Driver and TestNG on Eclipse
- Add a keyword in a Selenium automation framework and form an automated test case using keywords
- Building your own utilities for the Selenium automation framework
- Configuration and usage of the framework and run the automation suite

Before we dive into the chapter, let's take a quick look at what are the pros and cons of automation with framework and without framework.

Automation without framework

The following are the effects of automation without framework.

- The record/playback method increases the number of scripts
- Scripts are hardcoded
- Maintenance cost is too high
- It is difficult to trace scripts

Automation with Framework

The following are the effects of automation with framework.

- A set of industry standard best practices followed to support automation
- Break the testing activities and interrelate them to work as a whole
- The idea is to get efficient testing with reusability to avoid redundancy
- Making the workflow simpler, understandable, and easy to use

Test Automation Frameworks Evolution

Generation 1: Record/Playback
Generation 2: Action driven
Generation 3: Data driven
Generation 4: Keyword driven
Current Generation: Hybrid

Record/Playback

The test automation tool vendors market their product being able to capture user actions and later to playback. This is the basic paradigm for GUI-based automated regression testing—the so-called record/playback method (also called the capture/replay approach). It can be achieved using Selenium RC and Selenium IDE, but not with Selenium WebDriver.

Advantages

1. It is user friendly.

2. The user does not need to know scripting or programming languages.

Disadvantages

1. It is tool dependent.

2. There is no reusability factor.

3. The basic drawback in the record and playback methods is that scripts contain hardcoded data, hence parameterization is not possible. The costs associated with maintaining such scripts eventually become expensive and unacceptable.

4. The recorded scripts are not reliable, even if the application has not changed. They often fail on replay (pop-up windows, messages, IE display settings, and other things can happen that did not happen when the test was recorded).

5. If the tester makes an error entering data, the test must be re-recorded. If the application changes, the test must be re-recorded. All that is being tested are things that already work. Areas that have errors are encountered in the recording process (which is manual testing, after all). These bugs are reported, but a script cannot be recorded until the software is corrected. So, logically, nothing is tested with this approach.

6. There are no customized reports or logs. Users have to be dependent on the default features provided by the tool.

Action driven approach

The action-driven type of approach became possible with commercially available tools such as QTP/UFT or TestComplete, where each step or a group of reusable steps are converted into reusable actions and reused to form a test scenario.

Advantages

1. This is user friendly to some extent.

2. It's good to know basic scripting or a programming language but not mandatory.

3. Reusability is achieved.

Disadvantages

1. The action driven type of approach is tool dependent.
2. Reusability is achieved to some extent.
3. Data parameterization challenges still occur.
4. Reports and logs can be customized but this requires skill in using tools and scripting or knowledge of a programming language.
5. Scripts are heavy and become difficult to manage.

Data driven approach

A data-driven framework is the one in which the data is separated from scripts. Input data is passed from Excel, text, XML files, and even expected data is stored in an external file, such as text, Excel, and XML. Only necessary items such as browse, launch URL, login and navigation, and so on are written in the scripting/programming language supported by the automation tool. In the data driven approach, the scripts are called as drivers, which are driven by the data from the external source.

Advantages

1. Scripts can be developed at the stage of application development.
2. Since the data is separated from the scripts, the reusability of the same script with different combinations of data is possible.
3. Actual data and expected data can be well maintained in this approach, usually in Excel, text, XML files, and so on.
4. Usually, functions in this approach are developed in a way that it should return true/false, which leads to handling the errors properly and also increases the performance of the automation execution.

Disadvantages

1. The data driven type of approach requires some knowledge of the scripting or programming language used by the automation tool.
2. Since all the actual and expected data resides in external files such as txt, Excel, and XML, it results in maintaining multiple files and gets increased as and when the number of scripts increases. This leads to challenges in maintenance and more effort.

Keyword driven method

Some testers who know scripting with this tool will develop keywords and others frame automated tests using these keywords with the appropriate data. This requires the development of data sheet preparation. The automated test case looks exactly like a manual test case (provided that the keyword names are provided with a meaningful name). It uses a certain data-driven methodology as well.

In order to log on to an application, the following table is framed. This can be reused to log in to any application with different locators and inputs.

Keyword	Locator	Inputs	Wait (in seconds)
enterText	Id=Username	Testuser	
enterText	Id=Password	Testuser	
click	Id=Login		10
verify	Id=Logout	Logout	

Once the data table (data sheet) is ready, a master driver is written, which reads the data table and executes the respective keyword one by one based on the action provided on the data table. It also handles errors, writes step level execution information into logs, and generates summary reports.

Advantages

1. A detailed test plan is written in Excel, which contains keywords, actions, and data, which simulates the manual test cases. Hence, it is very easy to maintain and use.

2. The keywords are developed by a few people who are experts in automation tools and scripting and the rest can use the keywords and frame automation test cases in Excel without knowing the working of the automation tools and scripting language.

3. The tester needs to understand the keyword and the formats of the inputs that have to be provided for a respective keyword to form an automated test case, without knowing how the keyword is being built, they need not bother about scripting language.

4. If keywords are designed and planned well, then reusability is assured to the highest level.

Disadvantages

1. The development of keywords and generic utilities require scripting knowledge.

2. The tester has to understand and remember each and every keyword and the format of the input data provided. Initially, the tester has to be trained in the framework and keywords, which takes time, but later, we can see that a lot of time is saved through automation execution.

Hybrid

The most popularly used and implemented automation framework is *Data Driven + Keyword Driven*. The advantages of both the approaches, that is, data driven and keyword driven are combined to form a hybrid automation framework and the output is a very successful combination. Once the basic idea of a hybrid framework is implemented, it gets evolved by applying best practices based on the project needs to fetch better results and to bring the reusability factor to the highest degree.

The approach of data handling, that is, passing the data from outside the scripts, is taken from the Data Driven framework. The reusability factor of the utilities and keyword concept is taken from the Keyword Driven framework.

The following sections describe the prerequisites to be considered and the architecture design, framework structure, project folder structure, and implementation of the Hybrid Automation framework.

Environment specifications

- Selenium WebDriver (This supports all major browsers. We use Mozilla, Chrome, and IE.)
- Eclipse IDE
- Java
- TestNG

This framework has the following tools:

- Selenium WebDriver.
- Eclipse IDE: Eclipse is an **IDE (Integrated Development Environment)** for Java. The Eclipse IDE is the most popular product in the Eclipse open source project.
- TestNG: This is a testing framework inspired by JUnit and NUnit. It has extended new functionalities, which makes it more powerful and easier than the other testing frameworks.

The file formats used in the framework are as follows:

- **Excel files**: Test data is given through Excel spreadsheets
- **XML file**: Automation execution is triggered by `TestNG.XML`

Hybrid architecture design

The Hybrid framework contains both the Keyword Driven and Data Driven approaches incorporated in it. The Hybrid Automation architecture is as follows:

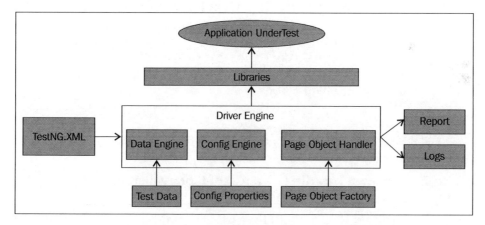

The explanation of each component of the framework design is as follows:

- **TestNG.XML**: This is an XML file used to trigger automation execution. It contains the application URL, build number, and so on.

- **Driver Engine**: Driver Engine in the framework is triggered by **TestNG. XML** to perform automation execution. It coordinates with each and every component of the framework and performs the automation execution starting from the beginning till the end, that is, it obtains the URL of the **AUT (Application Under Test)**, initiates the Selenium driver instance, reads the `Master.xls` file to know which test case to be executed, reads the data sheet, and executes the test case related keywords, data parameters, and so on.

  1. **Data Engine**: Data Engine is a part of **Driver Engine** that reads the test data related information and supplies the framework during execution.

  2. **Config Engine**: Config Engine is a part of **Driver Engine** that provides configuration related data to the framework during execution, for example, explicit waits for object, implicit waits, and so on.

  3. **Page Object Handler**: Page Object Handler is a part of **Driver Engine** that reads web element-related XPaths, IDs, names, and so on from **Page Object Factory**, which is required to identify the web object on the web page and convert that into a WebElement object. Later, the action on the objects will be taken care of by the respective keyword through utility functions.

- **Libraries**:

  1. **Java libraries**: It's a part of **Library** that contains a Java reference to the JAR files.

  2. **Selenium JAR files**: It's a part of **Library** that contains Selenium JAR files and browser-related drivers.

  3. **Utilities**: It's a part of **Library** that contains Java class files required in automation execution.

  4. **Application Specific Scripts**: It's a part of **Library** that contains application-specific Java class files, which is nothing but a keyword library.

- **Test Data**: Test Data contains automated test case-related data, that is, test case IDs, test case description, keyword, and the respective data parameters, and so on required for automation execution. This is controlled by **Data Engine**.

- **Configurations**: This contains the automation related configuration data. This is controlled by **Config Engine**.

- **Page Object Factory**: Page Object Factory contains web elements-related properties information such as XPaths, IDs, names, and so on, which is used to identify the object on a browser. This is controlled by **Page Object Handler**.

- **Reports**: This is a framework-generated HTML test case level report.

- **Logs**: It's user defined .txt format log files, containing every step level information on an executed automated test case. It is controlled by the **Utilities**.

The automation framework structure

Let's understand the various components of the Hybrid Automation framework in detail. Refer to the following diagram:

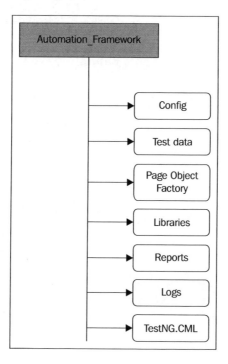

The explanation of each component of the Automation Framework structure is as follows:

1. **Config**: This contains automation-related configuration data.

2. **Testdata**: This contains following the Excel files:

    1. `Master.xls`: This file controls the test case execution.

    2. `GoogleSearchData.xls`: This file contains the test case related keywords and the data that will be executed.

3. **Page Object Factory**: The WebElement properties (XPath, name, ID, and so on) are defined in the Java class files in **Page Object Factory**.

4. **Libraries**: Libraries contain the following files:

    1. Java reference JAR files

    2. Selenium JAR files

    3. Application-specific Java class files

    4. Utilities Java class files required for automation execution

5. **Reports**: This is a framework generated HTML test case level report.

6. **Logs**: These are user defined `.txt` format log files, containing every step-by level executed information on an executed automated test case.

7. **TestNG.XML**: This is an XML file used to trigger automation execution. It contains the application URL, build number, and so on.

The project folder structure

The following is the automation framework structure when you view the entire framework through the **Navigator** view of the Eclipse IDE:

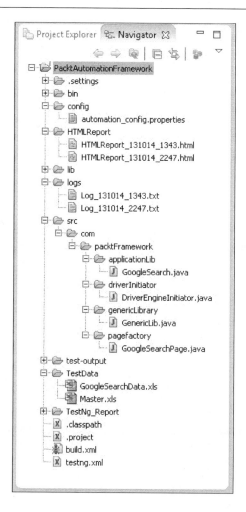

The explanation of each component of the `PacktAutomationFramework` project folder structure is as follows:

1. `config`: This has a properties file called `automation_config.properties`, which contains the automation related configuration data.

   The following code snippet is an example:

```
#Test data folder name (input data .xls files)
testDataFolder = TestData

#Master data excel file name (Master.xls file name)
masterxlsFileName = Master.xls
```

```
#Master data excel sheet name (Master.xls sheet name)
masterxlsSheetName = TestcaseList

#Application script java package name
scriptPackageName = com.packtFramework.applicationLib
```

2. `HTMLReport`: This folder contains the HTML reports of the automation execution.

   The following screenshot is an example:

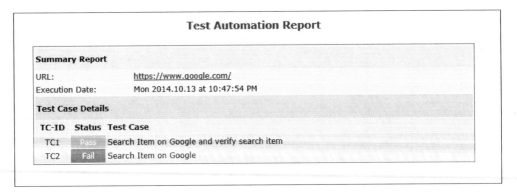

3. `Lib`: This is the library that contains the following files:
   - Java reference JAR files.
   - **Selenium JAR files**: You can find the Selenium-related JAR files at `http://docs.seleniumhq.org/download/`.
   - Application-specific Java class files.
   - Utility Java class files required for automation execution.
   - Framework-related JAR files.

The following screenshot is an example:

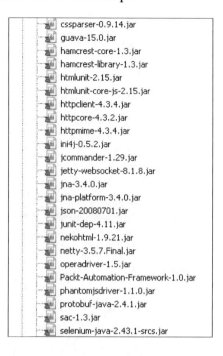

4. logs: This folder contains the logs of the automation execution. The results with respect to each step will be recorded here.

The following is an example of how the logs are recorded:

```
******************************************************************
*****************
TC Name:  [TC1]  Search Item on Google and verify search item
******************************************************************
*****************
------------------------------------------------------------------
-----------------
TestStep: [search]  Google Search
------------------------------------------------------------------
-----------------
10:48:18  [PASS]  Text packt publishing has been entered
successfully in webelement
10:48:18  [INFO]  search returns 'true' value

10:48:18  [TEST-STEP TIME]  0 Minute(s) 0 Second(s)
```

```
--------------------------------------------------------------------
------------------
TestStep: [verifyTitle]  Google Search verification
--------------------------------------------------------------------
------------------
10:48:23  [PASS]  packt publishing - Google Search verified
10:48:23  [INFO]  verifyTitle returns 'true' value

10:48:23  [TEST-STEP TIME]  0 Minute(s) 5 Second(s)
10:48:23  [TEST CASE TIME]  0 Hour(s) 0 Minute(s) 6 Second(s)
```

5. `src`: This folder contains the Java source files that belong to the automation framework and are application related. The folder structure (or package structure) of the `src` folder varies from company to company.

   An example of the Package structure is shown in the following screenshot:

As an example, we are considering the folders with the source files, which are shown in the following screenshot:

All source files will be saved in `\src\com\pactFramework\<respective folder>`.

Let's understand various folders under `packtFramework` and their purpose:

- `applicationLib`: The `applicationLib` folder in the `pactFramework` folder is used to store the Java class files related to application. For example, here, we have a java class file, `GoogleSearch.java`. Basically, all classes under `applicationLib` are constructors. They create instances of the following:

  1. **WebDriver**: This is a Selenium object.
  2. **log result**: It's an object to write logs.
  3. **utilities**: It's an object to use utilities to perform the generic `actionspage` factory object. It is an object to load Page Factory elements and it has an application under test-related methods (we call it as keywords).

  As an example, we have written two keywords:

  > **search**: This performs a Google search
  >
  > **verifyTitle**: This verifies the Google search results with respect to the title provided

- `driverInitiator`: The `driverInitiator` folder under `packtFramework` has a class called `DriverEngineInitiator` and is used for the following purposes:

  - It reads the URL of the application under test from `automation_config.properties`
  - It has a method called `testSetUp`, which accepts the URL as an argument
  - It has the starting execution point of the automation framework, that is, it uses `@test` annotation from TestNG
  - This initiates Selenium WebDriver
  - This initiates utilities required for generic actions
  - It interacts with **Driver Engine** of the framework

- `genericLibrary`: The `genericLibrary` folder under `packtFramework` has a class called `GenericLib` and is used for the following purposes:

  - All classes under `genericLibrary` are constructors
  - They create instances of WebDriver (it's a Selenium object) and log results (it's an object to write logs)
  - They contain generic utilities used to perform generic actions
  - The examples are clicking a button element, entering text into a edit field, selecting a checkbox, choosing a radio button from the radio group, and so on

We have two utilities for generic actions, `objClick` and `setEditField`

- ○ `objClick`: This requires WebElement as an argument. It performs the generic `click` action on WebElement, which is passed as an argument. `objClick` will check whether the WebElements is present on the web page or not. If WebElement is present, then it checks whether the WebElement present is `Enabled` for clicking or not. If WebElement is `Enabled`, then it performs a `click` action on WebElement and returns `True`. If any of the conditions fail before a `click` action, then it returns `False`.

- ○ `setEditField`: This requires two arguments, that is, WebElement and the string to input an edit field. It works as explained in the preceding utility, `objClick`.

- `pagefactory`: The `pagefactory` folder under `packtFramework` uses the Java class files to store the WebElement identification properties such as XPath, ID, name, and so on.

  Usually, each web page in an application under test will have one Java class file that stores the object identification properties and returns the web element.

  The following screenshot is an example:

```java
GoogleSearchPage.java

    package com.packtFramework.pagefactory;

  import org.openqa.selenium.WebElement;
    import org.openqa.selenium.support.FindBy;

    public class GoogleSearchPage {
        // ----------------------------------------------------------
        // XPaths and object names
        @FindBy(id="gbqfq")
        private WebElement searchTextfield;

        @FindBy(id="gbqfb")
        private WebElement searchButton;

        // ----------------------------------------------------------
        // Method Returning Web element
        public WebElement getSearchTextfield() {
            return searchTextfield;
        }

        public WebElement getSearchButton() {
            return searchButton;
        }
        // ----------------------------------------------------------
    }
```

The following table displays the details on how the `pagefactory` element is used along with the utility function:

Element	Function
`objGenericLib.setEditField(ObjGoog leSearchPage.getSearchTextfield(), sTestData);`	The `getSearchTextfield()` and `getSearchButton()` functions will return the WebElement, which is used to identify the web element on the AUT, and `setEditField`, `objClick` will perform generic actions on the WebElement identified.
`objGenericLib. objClick(ObjGoogleSearchPage. getSearchButton());`	

- `testdata`: This contains the following Excel spreadsheets:
  - `Master.xls`: This spreadsheet is used to control the test case execution

	Execution Status (Yes/No)	TestcaseID	Testcase Description	TestcaseDataFileName	TestcaseDataSheetName	
1						
2	YES	TC1	Search Item on Google and verify search item	GoogleSearchData	TCData	
3	YES	TC2	Search Item on Google	GoogleSearchData	TCData	

  - `GoogleSearchData.xls`: This spreadsheet contains the test case-related keywords and the data that will be executed

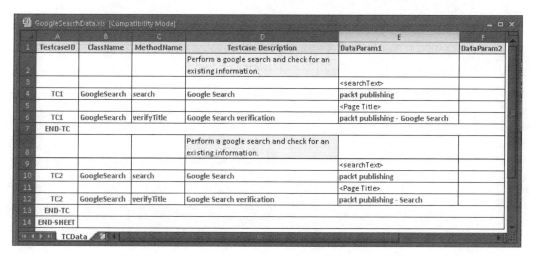

	TestcaseID	ClassName	MethodName	Testcase Description	DataParam1	DataParam2
1						
2				Perform a google search and check for an existing information.		
3					<searchText>	
4	TC1	GoogleSearch	search	Google Search	packt publishing	
5					<Page Title>	
6	TC1	GoogleSearch	verifyTitle	Google Search verification	packt publishing - Google Search	
7	END-TC					
8				Perform a google search and check for an existing information.		
9					<searchText>	
10	TC2	GoogleSearch	search	Google Search	packt publishing	
11					<Page Title>	
12	TC2	GoogleSearch	verifyTitle	Google Search verification	packt publishing - Search	
13	END-TC					
14	END-SHEET					

- `testng.xml`: This is an XML file used to trigger the automation execution. It contains the application URL, build number, and so on.

  The following code snippet is an example:

```xml
<?xml version="1.0" encoding="UTF-8"?>
<!DOCTYPE suite SYSTEM "http://testng.org/testng-1.0.dtd" >
<suite name="Automation">
  <test name="GoogleSearch">
    <parameter name="url"
      value="https://www.google.com/" />
    <classes>
  <class name="com.packtFramework.driverInitiator.
DriverEngineInitiator" />
    </classes>
  </test>
</suite>
```

Adding a keyword to a Selenium automation framework

Keywords are the building blocks of automation in the Hybrid Automation framework. They demonstrate that the piece is functionality tested and can be combined with another set of keywords in sequence to form a test scenario. Here, we can achieve the reusable factor to its highest degree. It's always a wise decision to choose and develop keywords. Let's understand how we develop a basic keyword and integrate it into a framework.

- Keywords are saved in the `applicationLib` folder of the framework
- Each class file in the `applicationLib` folder represents a module or a particular functionality of an application under test
- In the framework, we have the `GoogleSearch.java` class file
- In the `GoogleSearch.java` class file, we have a `GoogleSearch` class, which is a constructor

Let's understand the `search` keyword, which is used to perform a Google search:

```
-------------------------------------------------------------------
-----------
public boolean search(List<String> dataParamList) throws Exception {
  try {
    String sTestData = dataParamList.get(0);
    objGenericLib.setEditField
      (ObjGoogleSearchPage.getSearchTextfield(), sTestData);
```

```
    objGenericLib.objClick(ObjGoogleSearchPage.getSearchButton());
    return true;
} catch (Exception e) {
    return false;
  }
}
```


The following is a step-by-step explanation of the preceding code snippet:

1. **Keyword name**: search

2. **Return type**: Boolean (true or false)

3. **Arguments**: A search string (in an array called dataParamList)

4. Assign each element into a separate variable from an array, dataParamList, which will be used as an input on the objects on AUT, that is, String sTestData: dataParamList.get(0);

5. Pass the Page Object WebElement as an argument into a generic function, as shown here:

```
objGenericLib.setEditField
    (ObjGoogleSearchPage.getSearchTextfield(), sTestData);
objGenericLib.objClick
    (ObjGoogleSearchPage.getSearchButton());
```

6. If the step fails, the keyword will return false, indicating that you stop executing the test case, else it returns true, indicating that you execute the next keyword of the test case.

Form an automated test case using keywords

Assuming that we have keywords developed and we need to form an automated test case using the built keywords, let's understand how we can frame an automated test case by stitching the keywords being built. To do this, refer to the following steps:

1. Have a list of all the keywords under Java class files of the applicationLib folder of the framework.

2. Form an automated test case in a datasheet (as an example, GoogleSearchData.xls) by grouping the appropriate keywords (or methods).

3. Add the automated **TC** (**Test Case**) in Master.xls.

Steps to form an automated test case

This section will show you how to add an automated TC and add the TC info into `Master.xls`, which works as a controller for execution and also explains the significance of each and every column in the data and the master sheet.

The `packtAutomationFramework` folder has two data sheets, `Master.xls` and `GoogleSearchData.xls`. Both files are located in the `\PacktAutomationFramework\ TestData` project folder.

- Filling the `Master.xls` file:

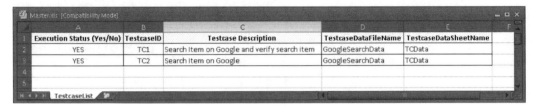

- ○ Column **A**: This shows the **Execution Status** of the test case. It can be either YES or NO.

- ○ Column **B**: This shows the **TestcaseID** of the test case. It is a unique ID for an automated test case.

- ○ Column **C**: The column **Testcase Description** shows a description of the respective automated test case.

- ○ Column **D**: The column **TestcaseDataFileName**, is a filename for the datasheet workbook where the automated test case is written, `GoogleSearchData.xls`.).

- ○ Column **E**: The column **TestcaseDataSheetName** is a filename for the datasheet where the automated test case is written under the Column **D** mentioned in the datasheet workbook, `TCData` in `GoogleSearchData.xls`.

All column header names are configured in `automation_config. properties`, as shown in the following code snippet:

```
# TestingType Option -- Regression
execution_status = Execution Status (Yes/No)

#Test data folder name (input data .xls files)
testDataFolder = TestData
```

```
#Master data excel file name (Master.xls file name)
masterxlsFileName = Master.xls

#Master data excel sheet name (Master.xls sheet name)
masterxlsSheetName = TestcaseList

#Master data Testcase Id (Master.xls Testcase Id)
masterDataTestcaseID = TestcaseID

#Master data Testcase Description (Master.xls Testcase
Description)
masterDataTestcaseDescription = Testcase Description

#Master data TestcaseDataFileName (Master.xls Testcase
DataFileName)
masterDataTestcaseDataFileName = TestcaseDataFileName
```

- Filling the datasheet `GoogleSearchData.xls` file:

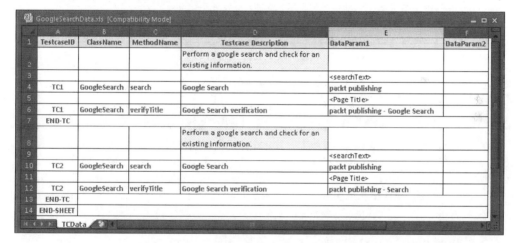

4. Column **A**: The **TestcaseID** column is a unique test case ID given to an automated test case, which gets matched from the `Master.xls` sheet at the time of execution.

5. Column **B**: The **ClassName** column is a class filename where the keyword (a method) belongs to.

6. Column **C**: The **MethodName** column is a keyword (or a method) that has to be executed under the test case.

7. Column D: The **Testcase Description** column is a description of the respective automated test case as well as the test step (a keyword or a method).

8. Column E onwards: **DataParam1** is a parameter required for a keyword (or a method) and the data is in the form of an array.

9. **END-TC** is a keyword that represents the end of the test case execution. Hence, **END-TC** needs to be mentioned for each and every test case.

10. The **END-SHEET** keyword represents the end of test suite execution. When test suite execution completes, the **END-SHEET** keyword needs to be mentioned at the end of the **TestcaseID** column to terminate the execution.

The **END-SHEET** and **END-TC** keyword names are configured in `automation_config.properties`, as shown in the following code snippet:

```
#Testcase excel data - end of each testcase
endTestCase = END-TC
#Testcase excel data - end of testcase data sheet
endDataSheet = END-SHEET
```

Building your own utilities for the Selenium automation framework

This section will guide you to develop the utilities for a Hybrid Automation framework which was built in the earlier stages in this chapter. The utilities are the functions that perform generic actions across the automation execution, for example, `objClick`. The details are explained as follows:

- Utilities are saved in the `genericLibrary` folder of the framework, which is saved in the `packtFramework` folder of the framework

- In the framework, we have the `GoogleSearch.java` class file

- In the `GenericLib.java` class file, we have a `GenericLib` class, which is a constructor

Let's understand the `objClick` utility, which is used to perform a click action on any object type = Button:

```
-------------------------------------------------------------------
-----------
public boolean objClick(WebElement element) throws Exception {
try {
```

```
if (element != null) {
element.click();
return true;
}
LogResult.fail("Element not found to click on element having xpath " +
element);
return false;
} catch (Exception e) {
LogResult.fail("Error occurred while clicking on element having xpath
" + element);
return false;
}
}
```

The following is a step-by-step explanation of the preceding code snippet:

1. **Utility name**: `objClick`

2. **Return type**: `Boolean` (`true` or `false`)

3. **Arguments**: WebElement of the object type: web button

4. Pass the Page Object WebElement as an argument into a generic function, as shown in the following lines of code:

    ```
    objGenericLib.setEditField(ObjGoogleSearchPage.
    getSearchTextfield(), sTestData);
    objGenericLib.objClick(ObjGoogleSearchPage.getSearchButton());
    ```

5. If the step fails, the keyword will return `false`, indicating that you stop executing the test case, else it returns `true`, indicating that you execute the next keyword of the test case.

The code snippet works as follows:

1. The `objClick` utility checks whether WebElement is present on the web page or not.

2. If WebElement is present, then it checks whether WebElement is **Enabled** for clicking or not.

3. If WebElement is **Enabled**, then it performs a `click` action on the WebElement and returns `true`.

4. If any of the conditions fail before a **click** action, then it returns `false`.

The following steps are to be considered before and after you execute an automation:

1. Identify tasks that an application has to accomplish.
2. Collect the set of necessary input data that has to be created.
3. Expected results have to be defined so that one can judge that an application (a requested feature) works correspondingly.
4. Automation tool executes a test.
5. Compares the expected results with actual results, and decides whether the test has been passed successfully.

Configuration and usage of the framework

The following are the steps for configuring the framework:

1. Launch Eclipse
2. Import the `packtAutomationFramework` framework as **Existing project**.
3. Enable the **Navigator** view on Eclipse (from **Window | Show View**).
4. Right-click on `testing.xml` and run as **TestNG Suite**.

Run the automation suite

The following are the steps to run the automation suite:

1. Provide the URL in a `testing.xml` (`\PacktAutomationFramework\testng.xml`):

   ```
   <parameter name="url" value="https://www.google.com/" />
   ```

2. Set **Execution Status** to **YES** for the test cases you want to run in the file at the location, `\PacktAutomationFramework\TestData\Master.xls`.
3. Right-click on `testing.xml` and run as **TestNG Suite**.

Execution starts and ends

The following are the steps for starting and ending the execution:

1. Go to `\PacktAutomationFramework\logs` and find the log file for test case step level analysis.
2. Go to `\PacktAutomationFramework\HTMLReport` for HTML summary results.

Summary

We learned the following points related to framework:

- Why the Automation framework is required and what happens without automation framework

- The evolution of frameworks and analysis, from record and playback to hybrid frameworks

- Understanding the Hybrid Automation framework in detail, including its architecture, design, and implementation of the Hybrid Automation framework using the Page Object factory concept using Selenium—WebDriver and TestNG on Eclipse

- How to add a keyword into a Selenium automation framework and how to create an automated test case in a datasheet

- How to build a generic function or utilities for the Selenium automation framework

- Configuration and usage of the framework and run the automation suite with results and log analysis

Self-test questions

1. Which one is the latest generation of framework type?
   a. Data Driven
   b. Keyword
   c. Hybrid
   d. None

2. What does the Page Object factory store?
   a. Object identification properties
   b. WebElements
   c. Both a and b
   d. None of the above

3. Automation execution is triggered through:
   a. Master.xls
   b. Testing.xml
   c. Build.xml
   d. None of the above

4. Automation execution is triggered through?

    a. `Master.xls`

    b. `Testing.xml`

    c. `Build.xml`

    d. `None of the above`

5. Application-related methods or keywords are stored in?

    a. `applcationLib`

    b. `genericLib`

    c. `Either a or b`

    d. `None of the above`

6. `objClick` is an?

    a. `Utility`

    b. `keyword`

    c. `Either a or b`

    d. `None of the above`

8
Mobile Devices

We are currently seeing an explosion of mobile devices in the market. A lot of them are more powerful than your average computer was just over a decade ago. This means that in addition to having nice, clean, responsive, and functional desktop applications, we are starting to ensure the same basic functionality is available to mobile devices. In this chapter, we will be looking at how we can set up mobile devices to be used with Selenium WebDriver.

In this chapter, we will learn:

- How to use the stock browser on Android
- How to test with Opera mobile
- How to test on iOS

So, let's get on with it.

While you can use the Android emulator for the Android parts of this chapter, it is highly recommended that you have a real device that you can use. The reason is that the emulator tries to emulate the hardware that the phones run on. This means that it needs to translate it to a low-level command that ARM-based devices will understand. A real iOS device is not needed since we are using a simulator, which will be faster when compared to a real iOS device. The device will also need to have Android 4.0+, or better known as **Ice Cream Sandwich**. You will need to download the Android app from `http://code.google.com/p/selenium/downloads/list`. It will be named `android-server-<version>.apk`, where `<version>` is the latest version.

You will however need to have a machine with OS X on to start the simulator since it is part of Xcode. If you do not have Xcode installed, you can download it via the AppStore. You will also need to install all of the command-line tools that come with Xcode. You will also need to check out the Selenium code from its source repository. You will need to build the WebDriver code for iOS since it can't be added to the Apple App Store to be downloaded onto devices.

Working with Android

Android devices are becoming a commonplace with owners of smartphones and tablets. This is because there are a number of handset providers in the market. This has meant that in some parts of the world, it is the only way that some people can access the Internet. With this in mind, we need to make sure that we can test the functionality.

Emulator

While it is not recommended that you use the emulator due to the speed of it, it can be really useful. Since it will act like a real device in that it will run all the bits of code that we want on the virtual device, we can see how a web application will react.

Creating an emulator

If you do not have an Android device that you can use for testing, then you can set up an Android emulator. The emulator will then get the Selenium WebDriver APK installed and then that will control the browser on the device. Before we start, you will need to download the Android SDK from `http://developer.android.com/sdk/index.html`.

 The AVDs can be managed from the Command Prompt. Refer to `http://developer.android.com/tools/devices/managing-avds-cmdline.html` for more information.

The following steps are used in creating and running an emulator in an Android SDK:

1. Open up Command Prompt or a terminal.
2. Enter `cd <path>/android-sdk/tools`, where `<path>` is the path to the `android-sdk` directory.
3. Now, enter `android create avd -n my_android -t 14`, where:
   - The `-n my_android` command gives the emulator the name `my_android`.
   - The `-t 14` command tells it which version of Android to use. `14` and higher is Android `4.0` and higher support.

4. When prompted **Do you wish to create a custom hardware profile [no]**, enter **no**.

5. Run the emulator with the following command line:

```
emulator -avd my_android
```

It will take some time to come up, but once it has been started, you will not have to restart unless it crashes or you purposefully close it. Once loaded, you should see something like the following screenshot:

We have just seen what is involved in setting up the Android emulator that we can use for testing of mobile versions of our applications. As was mentioned, we need to make sure that we set up the emulator to work with Android 4.0 or later. For the emulator we need to have a target platform of 14 or later. Now that we have this done, we can have a look at installing the WebDriver Server on the device.

Installing the Selenium WebDriver Android Server

We saw that we can access different machines and control the browsers on those machines with Selenium WebDriver RemoteDriver. We need to do the same with Android. The APK file that you downloaded earlier is the Selenium Server that is specifically designed for Android devices. It has a smaller memory footprint since mobile devices do not have the same amount of memory as your desktop machine.

We need to install this on the emulator or the physical device that you have.

Installing the Android Server

In this section, we will learn the steps required to install the Android server on the device or emulator that you are going to be using. To do this, you will need to have downloaded the APK file from `http://code.google.com/p/selenium/downloads/list`. If you are installing this onto a real device, make sure that you allow installs from **Unknown Sources**. The following steps are used to install the Android Server:

1. Open Command Prompt or a terminal.
2. Start the emulator or device if you haven't already.
3. We need to run the available devices:

   `<path to>/android_sdk/platform-tools/adb devices`

4. It will look like the following screenshot:

   ```
   * daemon not running. starting it now on port 5037 *
   * daemon started successfully *
   List of devices attached
   3930A259826000EC          device
   ```

5. Take the serial number of the device (for emulator, `serialid` = `emulator-xxxx`).
6. Now, we will need to install the Android SDK with the following command:

   `adb -s <serialId> -e install -r  android-server.apk`

7. Once this is done, you will see this in Command Prompt or the terminal:

   ```
   3594 KB/s (1881490 bytes in 0.511s)
           pkg: /data/local/tmp/android-server-2.21.0.apk
   Success
   ```

8. And on the device, you will see the following screenshot:

We just saw how we can install the Android Server on the server. This process is useful for installing any Android app from the command line. Now that this is done, we are ready to start looking at running some Selenium WebDriver code against the device.

Creating a test for Android

Now that we have looked at getting the device or emulator ready, we are ready to start creating a test that will work against a site. The good thing about the Selenium WebDriver, like Selenium RC, is that we can easily move from browser to browser with only a small change. In this section, we will be introduced to the AndroidDriver.

Using the Android driver

In this section, we will be looking at running some tests against an Android device or emulator. This should be a fairly simple change to our test, but there are a couple of things that we need to do right before the test runs:

1. Open Command Prompt or a terminal.

2. We need to start the server. The syntax for starting the server is as follows:

```
adb shell am start -a android.intent.action.MAIN -n
<package>/<activity class>
```

3. We can do this by touching the app or we can do this from the command line with the following command:

```
db shell am start -a android.intent.action.MAIN -n
```

4. We now need to forward all the HTTP traffic to the device or emulator. This means that all the JSON Wire Protocol calls, that we learnt earlier, go to the device. We do it with the following line of code:

```
adb -s <serialId> forward tcp:8080 tcp:8080
```

5. Now, we are ready to update our test. I will show an example from the previous test. The code is shown as follows:

```java
import junit.framework.TestCase;

import org.openqa.selenium.By;
import org.openqa.selenium.WebElement;
import org.openqa.selenium.android.AndroidDriver;


public class TestChapter7 {

  WebDriver driver;

  @Before
  public void setUp(){
     driver = new AndroidDriver();
     driver.get("http://book.theautomatedtester.co.uk/chapter4");
  }

  @After
  public void tearDown(){
     driver.quit();
  }

  @Test
  public void testExamples(){
     WebElement element = driver.findElement(By.id("nextBid"));
     element.sendKeys("100");
  }
}
```

6. Run the test. You will see that it runs the same test against the Android device. In *Chapter 7, Automation Framework Development and Building Utilities*, we had this work against desktop browsers.

We just ran our first test against an Android device. We saw that we had to forward the HTTP traffic to port 8080 to the device. This means that the normal calls, which use the JSON Wire Protocol, will then be run on the device.

Currently, Opera software is working on getting OperaDriver to work on mobile devices. There are a few technical details that are being worked on, and hopefully, in the future we will be able to use it.

Mozilla is also working on their solution for mobile with Selenium. Currently, a project called Marionette is being worked on, which allows Selenium to work on Firefox OS, Firefox Mobile for Android, and Firefox for Desktop. You can read up on this at `https://wiki.mozilla.org/Auto-tools/Projects/Marionette`.

Updating tests for Android
Have a look at updating all of the tests that you have written so far in the book to run on Android. It should not take you long to update them.

Running with OperaDriver on a mobile device

In this section, we will have a look at using the OperaDriver and Selenium WebDriver object to control Opera, in order to drive Opera Mobile. Opera has a large market share on mobile devices, especially on lower-end Android devices.

Before we start, we will need to download a special emulator for Opera Mobile.

As of writing this, it has just come out of Opera's labs, so the download links may have been updated.

For Windows: `http://www.opera.com/download/get.pl?id=349 69&sub=true&nothanks=yes&location=360`

For Mac: `http://www.opera.com/download/get. pl?id=34970&sub=truen=360`

For Linux 64 bit Deb: `http://www.opera.com/download/get.pl?i d=34967&sub=truyes&location=360`

Tarball version for Linux 64 bit Deb: `http://www.opera.com/ download/get.pl?id=34968&sub=trion=360`

Linux 32 bit Deb version: `http://www.opera.com/download/get. pl?id=34965&sub=t&nothanks=yes&locatioe&nothanks=ue&no thanks=yes&locatrue&nothanks=yes&location=360`

TarBall version for Linux 32 bit Deb: `http://www.opera.com/ download/get.pl?id=34966&sub=true&nothanks=yes&locati on=360`

Let's now see this in action.

Using OperaDriver on Opera Mobile

To make sure that we have the right amount of coverage over the browsers that users may be using, there is a good chance that you will need to add Opera Mobile. Before starting, make sure that you have downloaded the version of the emulator for your Operating System with one of the links mentioned previously. Create a new test file. Add the following code to it:

```
import junit.framework.TestCase;

import org.openqa.selenium.By;
import org.openqa.selenium.WebElement;

public class TestChapter7OperaMobile{
  WebDriver driver;
}
```

1. What we now need to do is add a setup method. We will have to add a couple of items to our `DesiredCapabilities` object. This will tell OperaDriver that we want to work against a mobile version. Refer to the following steps:

```
@Before
public void setUp(){
  DesiredCapabilities c = DesiredCapabilities.opera();
  c.setCapability("opera.product", OperaProduct.MOBILE);
  c.setCapability("opera.binary",
    "/path/to/my/custom/opera-mobile-build");

  driver = new OperaDriver(c);
}
```

2. Now, we can add a test to make sure that we have a working test again:

```
@Test
public void testShouldLoadGoogle() {
  driver.get("http://www.google.com");
  //Let's find an element to see if it works
  driver.findElement(By.name("q"));
}
```

3. Let's now add a `teardown` function:

```
@After
public void teardown(){
  driver.quit();
}
```

4. Your class altogether should look like the following:

```
import junit.framework.TestCase;

import org.openqa.selenium.By;
import org.openqa.selenium.WebElement;

public class TestChapter7OperaMobile{
  WebDriver driver;

  @Before
  public void setUp(){
    DesiredCapabilities c = DesiredCapabilities.opera();
    c.setCapability("opera.product", OperaProduct.MOBILE);
    c.setCapability("opera.binary",
      "/path/to/my/custom/opera-mobile-build");

    driver = new OperaDriver(c);
  }

  @After
  public void teardown(){
    driver.quit();
  }
  @Test
  public void testShouldLoadGoogle() {
    driver.get("http://book.theautomatedtester.co.uk");

  }
}
```

5. The following screenshot should appear in your emulator:

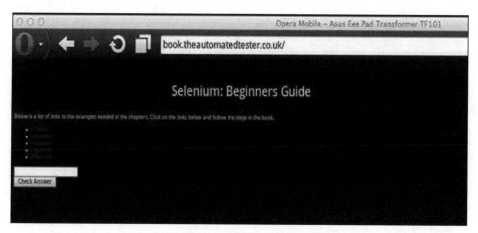

We just saw what is required to run a test against Opera Mobile using OperaDriver. This uses the same communication layer that is used for communicating with the Opera desktop browser called Scope.

We will see the mobile versions of web applications, if they are available, and be able to interact with them.

If you would like the OperaDriver to load up tablet size UI, then you can add the following code to use the tablet UI with a display of 1280 x 800 pixels. This is a common size for tablets that are currently on the market:

```
c.setCapability("opera.arguments",
  "-tabletui -displaysize 1280x800");
```

If you want to see the current orientation of the device and access the touchscreen elements, you can swap the OperaDriver object for OperaDriverMobile. For the most part, you should be able to do nearly all of your work against the normal driver.

Working with iOS

iPhones and iPod Touches are such commonplace these days. A lot of companies are working hard to offer a really good experience for these users. This means that users are starting to become accustomed to using web applications with their phones.

We can run our tests against the simulator or against the real device. Compared to Android, the simulator is really quick. This is because it is not trying to emulate the hardware of actual Apple devices.

Setting up the simulator

In this section, we will be making sure that we have the simulator or device ready. To do this, we will need to do the following steps:

1. If you haven't checked the Selenium code out, follow the steps at
    `http://code.google.com/p/selenium/source/checkout`.

2. Refer to the following link for a complete iOS simulation guide:
    `https://developer.apple.com/library/mac/documentation/IDEs/Conceptual/iOS_Simulator_Guide/`

3. Open `selenium/iphone/iWebDriver.xcodeproj` in XCode.

4. If you want to build it for the simulator, set your build configuration to **Simulator | iPad OS 5.0 | iWebDriver**. This is done in a drop-down box in the top-left of the **Project** window.

5. Click **Build & Go!**.The iWebDriver instance will be built and the simulator will start. You can see what it will look like in the following screenshot:

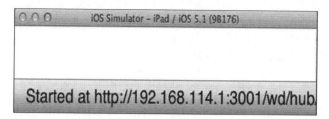

We just got all the requirements ready to start writing our first test. After making sure that we have XCode, which has the iOS SDK, we were able to start the simulator and have iWebDriver installed.

We will now have a look at how to set up running your tests against a real device. Before we do that, we will have to make sure that we have set up a provisioning profile.

To do this, we need to do the following. One thing to note is that you will have to pay 99 USD to join the iOS program. To do this, try the following steps:

1. Get a developer account from Apple. This is done at `https://developer.apple.com`.

2. Create a certificate signing request.

3. Open **Keychain Access**:

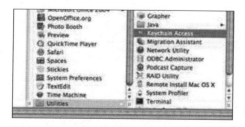

4. Request a certificate from a certificate authority by navigating to **Keychain Access | Certificate Assistant | Request a Certificate From a Certificate Authority**:

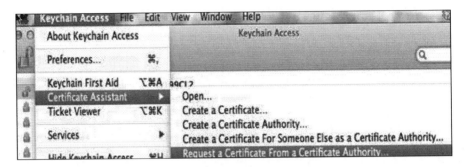

5. Complete the form as show in the following screenshot:

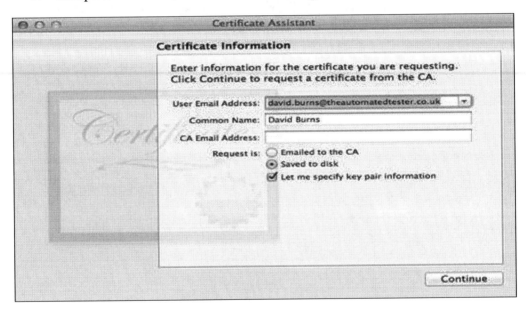

6. Click **Continue** and then save the file to a place where you'll be able to access it:

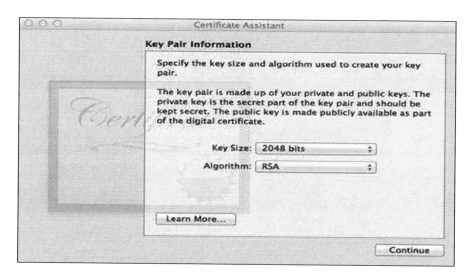

7. Click **Continue** and then it should say that it was successful, as shown in the following screenshot:

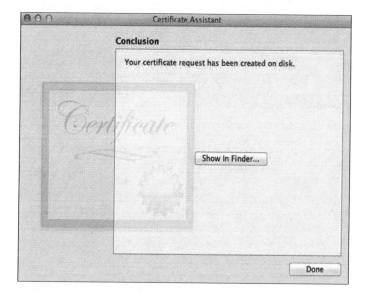

8. Go to the iPhone Developer Program portal on
   `https://developer.apple.com`.

9. Launch the **Assistant**, as in the following screenshot:

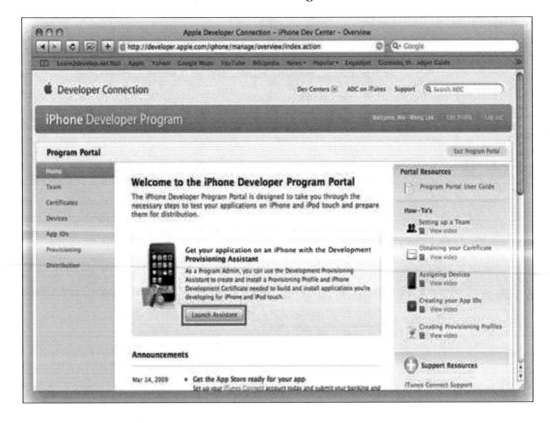

10. Go through the **Provisioning Assistant** and complete all the steps that you are asked to do:

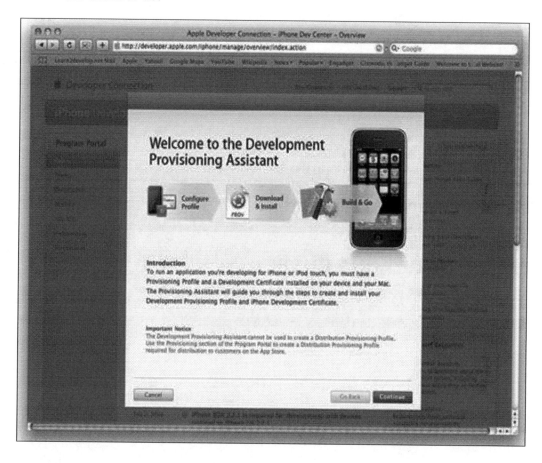

Setting up on a real device

Setting up tests to run on a simulator is quite useful, but having the tests running on a mobile device can be really useful. Let's have a look at setting this up on a real mobile device.

You will also need a provisioning profile from Apple to be installed and configured for your device.

1. Open `Info.plist` and edit the `Bundle Identifier` to `com.NAME.${PRODUCT_NAME:identifier}`, where `NAME` is the name you registered your provisioning profile to be an authority on.

2. Make sure your device is connected to your computer. Your device must also be routable from your computer. The easiest way to do this is to configure a Wi-Fi network and connect your device to it.

3. Click **Build & Go!**. iWebDriver will be installed on the device.

We have just installed iWebDriver on a real device. We can now run our tests against iPhones or iPads. The hard part in running tests against these devices is now done. Let's have a look at updating our tests.

Creating a test for iOS devices

Now that we have looked at getting the device or simulator ready, we are ready to start creating a test that will work against a site. The good thing about the Selenium WebDriver, like Selenium RC, is that we can easily move from browser to browser with only a small change. In this section, we will be introduced to the iPhoneDriver.

Using the iPhone driver

In this section, we will be looking at running some tests against an iOS device or simulator. This should be a fairly simple change to our test, but there are a couple of things that we need to do right before the test runs.

Now, we are ready to update our test. I will show an example from the previous test:

```
import junit.framework.TestCase;

import org.openqa.selenium.By;
import org.openqa.selenium.WebElement;
import org.openqa.selenium.iphone.IphoneDriver;

public class TestChapter7 {

  WebDriver driver;

  @Before
  public void setUp(){
    driver = new IPhoneDriver();
    driver.get("http://book.theautomatedtester.co.uk/chapter4");
  }

  @After
  public void tearDown(){
    driver.quit();
  }
```

```
@Test
public void testExamples(){
  WebElement element = driver.findElement(By.id("nextBid"));
  element.sendKeys("100");
  }
}
```

Run the test. You will see that it runs the same test against an iOS device. In *Chapter 7, Automation Framework Development and Building Utilities*, we had this work against desktop browsers.

We have just seen how we can run our tests against iOS devices. Depending on the simulator we start XCode from, we can either have it run against iPhone or iPad.

Updating tests for iOS devices

Have a look at updating all of the tests that you have written so far in the book to run on iOS. It should not take you long to update them.

Summary

We learned a lot in this chapter about using Selenium WebDriver with mobile devices. We saw that after a little setup of the device and the machine running the test, it was fairly easy to get up and running.

Specifically, we covered the following topics:

- **Working with Android**: In this section, we had a look at what is needed to set up Android for testing with Selenium WebDriver. We set up an emulator in case we didn't have a real device. We also saw how we can install the Android Server on the device or emulator.

  We then moved on to creating our test that ran against the emulator or the device.

- **Working with iOS**: In this section, we looked at setting up the simulator or getting iWebDriver installed on a real device.

Now that we've learnt about mobile web testing, let's have a look at really setting up the Selenium Grid—which is the topic of the next chapter.

Self-test questions

1. How do we set up an Android emulated device for our tests?

2. How do you see which devices are connected to the host?

    a. adb devices

    b. Adb phones

    c. Adb handsets

3. How do you install the APK on the device or emulator?

    a. `adb -s <serialId> -e install -r  android-server.apk`

    b. Install it from `http://code.google.com/p/selenium/downloads/list`

    c. both

4. How do you start the app on the emulator or device without touching it?

5. How do I forward the HTTP traffic to the device?

    a. `Abd -s <serialId> redirect tcp:8080 tcp:8080`

    b. `Abd -s <serialId> redirect tcp:8080 tcp:8080`

    c. `adb -s <serialId> forward tcp:8080 tcp:8080`

9
Getting Started with the Selenium Grid

In this chapter, we will have a look at what Selenium Grid is and how we can set it up on different environments. All tests are stored in a common location and we need not worry about any environment changes since all are pointing to the same located tests.

In this chapter, we will learn about the following topics:

- Setting up the Selenium Grid hub
- Setting up the Selenium Grid **Remote Control (RC)**
- Creating tests for the grid
- Running tests in parallel

So, let's get on with it.

 Please make sure that you download the latest Selenium server from `http://seleniumhq.org/download`.

Understanding Selenium Grid

Selenium Grid is a version of Selenium that allows teams to set up a number of Selenium instances and then have one central point to send your Selenium commands to. This differs from what we saw in Selenium Remote WebDriver, where we always have to explicitly say where the Selenium server is as well as know what browsers that server can handle.

With Selenium Grid, we just ask for a specific browser, and then the hub that is part of Selenium Grid will route all the Selenium commands through the Remote Control you want. Refer to the following diagram for the interaction between the Selenium Grid hub and the other components:

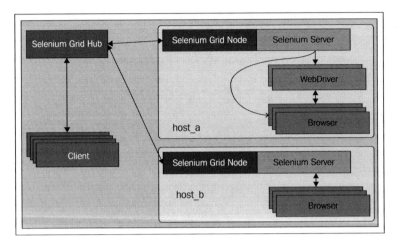

Selenium Grid also allows us to call a specific browser on a specific platform with just a simple update to the desired capabilities object that we learned about in the previous chapters. This allows us to route our tests accordingly so that we know that we are testing on the right browser and on the right platform. We can see an example of this in the following screenshot:

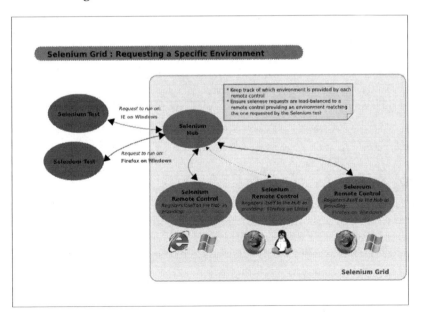

We will see how to create tests for this later in the chapter, but for now, let's have a look at making sure we have all the necessary items ready for the grid.

We are now ready to start setting up the grid.

The Selenium Grid hub

Selenium Grid works by having a central point that tests can connect to, and then commands are pushed to Selenium Server nodes that are connected to the hub. The hub has a web interface that tells you about the Selenium Server and the browser instances connected to the hub, and if they are currently in use.

Launching the hub

Now that we are ready to start working with Selenium Grid, we need to set up the grid. This is a simple command that we run in the console or Command Prompt.

1. Open Command Prompt or a console.

2. Run the following command:

   ```
   java -jar selenium-server-standalone-x.xx.xx.jar -role hub
   ```

3. When that command executes, you should see something like the following screenshot:

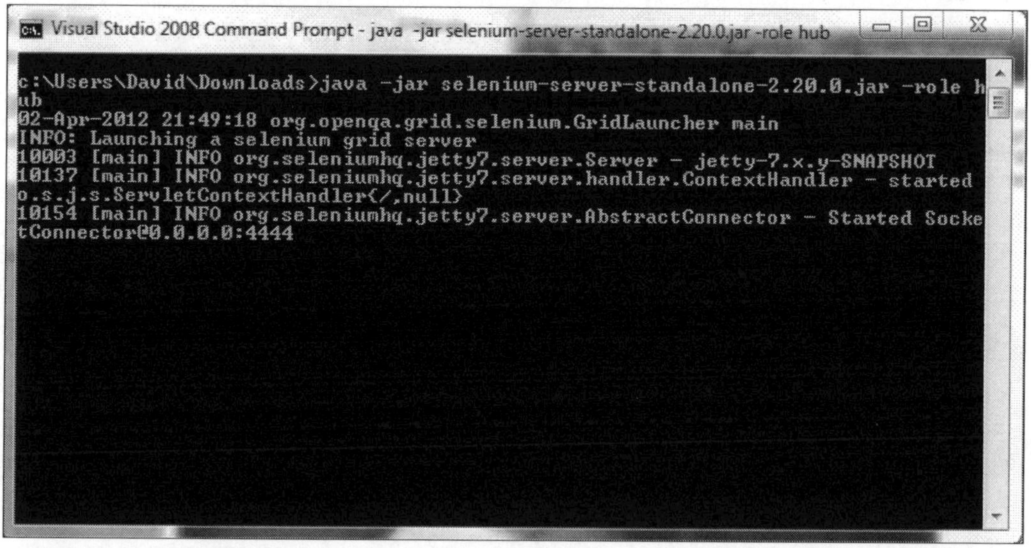

4. We can see that this is running in Command Prompt or the console. We can also see the hub running from within a browser.

5. We can enter `http://nameofmachine:4444/grid/console` where `nameofmachine` is the name of the machine with the hub. If it is on your machine, then you can enter `http://localhost:4444/grid/console`. Refer to the following screenshot for the output:

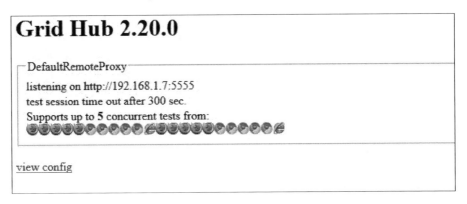

We have successfully started Selenium Grid Hub. This is the central point of our tests and Selenium Grid instances. We saw that when we started Selenium Grid, it showed us which items were available according to the configuration file that is with the normal install. One thing to note is that if you need to change the port, you can pass in `-port ####`. Just replace the `####` with the port number that you wish to use.

We then had a look at how we can see what the grid is doing by having a look at the hub in a browser. We did this by putting the URL `http://nameofmachine:4444/grid/console` where `nameofmachine` is the name of the machine that we would like to access with the hub. It shows what configured environments the hub can handle, what grid instances are available, and which instances are currently active.

Now that we have the hub ready we can have a look at starting up instances.

Adding instances to the hub

Now that we have successfully started the Selenium Grid hub, we will need to have a look at how we can start adding Selenium servers to the hub so that it starts forming the grid of computers that we are expecting. You will notice that compared to Selenium Grid for Selenium 1, we won't have to add a new server for each browser that we want to use. The server has always been able to handle more than one browser and because of architectural changes, we can now start one server and have it control all the browsers installed on that machine.

Adding a server with the defaults

In this section, we will launch Selenium Server and get it to register with the hub. We will assume that the browser on which you will like to register all known browsers and the hub are on the same machine as the grid node. We will pass in two required arguments: that the server we are starting is a node, and the location of the hub. The Selenium Server will try and use the 5555 port. If this is not available, you will get an error saying that the port is already in use. We can, and will in a future section, see how you can set the port manually. Refer to the following steps:

1. Open Command Prompt or the console.

2. Enter the `java -jar selenium-server-standalone-2.20.0. jar -role node -hub http://localhost:4444/grid/register` command and press **return**. You should see the following in your Command Prompt or the console:

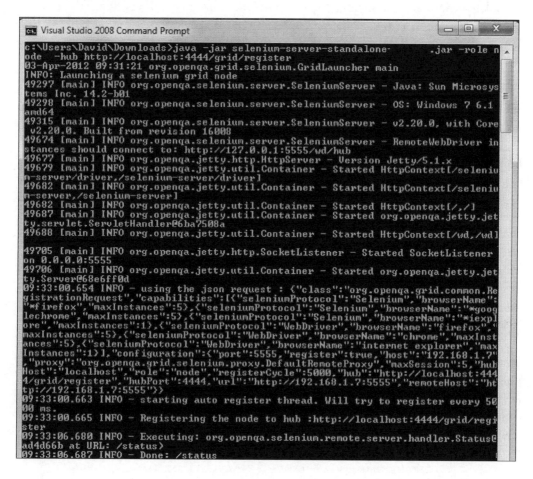

3. You will see this in the Selenium Grid hub site as the following screenshot:

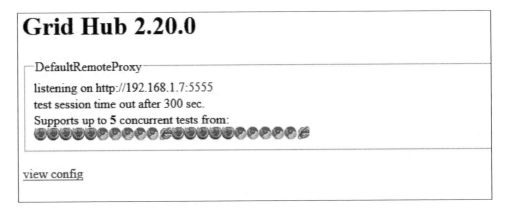

We have added our first machine to our own Selenium Grid. It has used all the defaults that are available. It has created a Selenium Server instance that will take any Firefox, Google Chrome, and in this case, Internet Explorer requests and is on the same machine as the host of Selenium Server grid. This is a useful way to set up the grid really quickly with all the default browsers.

Adding Selenium Remote Control for different machines

Selenium Grid is a very powerful tool when you add it to multiple operating systems. This allows us to check that, for instance, whether Firefox on Windows and Firefox on Linux is doing the same thing during a test. To register new remote controls to the grid from a machine other than the one hosting the hub, we need to tell it where the hub is.

Let's see this in action.

Selenium Server for different machines

For this section, you will need to have another machine available for you to use. This can be the Ubuntu machine that you needed for the previous chapter. If you have a small grid, then you can name it according to the operating system that it is running on.

1. Open Command Prompt or a console.
2. Run the `java -jar selenium-server-standalone.jar -role node -hub http://<name of server>:4444/grid/register` command.

3. When you have run this, your grid site should look like the following:

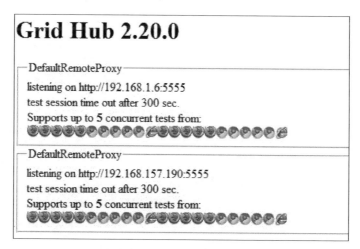

We have added a new remote control to the grid from a machine other than where the Selenium Grid Hub is running. This is the first time that we have been able to set up our remote control instances in a grid. We learned about the –hub argument that is needed when launching the Selenium Server. We then saw that it has updated the grid site, which is running on the hub.

Now that we have this working as we expected, let's have a look at setting up the server to do specific tasks.

Adding Selenium Server to do specific browser tasks on specific operating systems

Selenium Grid is extremely powerful when we start using different browsers on the grid, since we can't run all the different browsers on a single machine due to operating systems and browser combinations. There are currently up to nine different combinations that are used by most people, so getting Selenium Grid to help with this can give you the test coverage that you need.

To do this, we pass in the –browser argument in a command-line call. Let's see how we can set the items.

Setting the environment when starting Selenium Remote Control

Now that we need to get Internet Explorer Selenium Remote Controls added to our grid, we have to add the `-browser` argument to our call with the target on the configured environments. Since we want to use Internet Explorer, we can use the IE on the Windows target:

1. Open a console or Command Prompt.

2. Run the following command:

    ```
    java -jar selenium-server-standalone.jar -role node  -hub http://
    localhost:4444/grid/register -browser browserName="internet
    explorer",maxInstances=1,platform=WINDOWS
    ```

3. When the preceding command is running, your hub page should look like this:

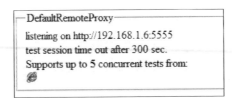

We just saw how we can create grid nodes to only have the browsers that we want. We chose Internet Explorer, but we can also choose Firefox, Google Chrome, or Opera. This is quite useful when we need to test a large amount of browser and operating system combinations. If you enter `-browser` on the command line, it will add the browsers too.

Using Selenium Grid 1 with your YAML file

If you have been using Selenium Grid from Selenium 1, you will have set up your YAML file. This can now be used with Selenium by passing in a file like the following one. To do this, we just need to pass in a new argument called `-grid1Yml`:

```
hub:
  port: 4444
  remoteControlPollingIntervalInSeconds: 180
  sessionMaxIdleTimeInSeconds: 300
  environments:
    - name:     "Firefox on Windows"
      browser: "*firefox"
```

Using Selenium Grid 1 configuration

A number of us have set up a Selenium Grid using the Selenium 1 Grid and have been using it for a long time. Since we have this, why not upgrade the nodes to Selenium Server that supports both Remote Control and WebDriver and use our original configuration? One thing to note is that we will only be able to run Selenium Remote Control tests this way.

Let's have a try at starting all this up:

1. Open a console or Command Prompt.
2. Run the following command:

    ```
    java -jar selenium-server-standalone.jar -role hub -grid1Yml
    selenium-grid-1.0.8/grid_configuration.yml
    ```

3. If we have a look at the grid `config` page by clicking the view `config` link, then we will see it in there:

We just got Selenium Grid to load our original Selenium Grid item by passing in the original YAML file. This then gets used by the hub once it has started up!

Running tests against the grid

Now that we have set up the grid with different instances, we should have a look at how we can write tests against these remote controls on the grid. We can pass in the value of the target that we can see in the grid and then run the tests. So instead of passing in the standard desired capabilities, you can be more specific and the grid hub will route data so that you can then run the tests as normal. Let's see this in action.

Writing tests against the grid

Now that we have a Selenium Grid set up, we need to write a test that works against the grid. Working against Selenium Grid is exactly the same as working with Selenium WebDriver's RemoteWebDriver. The Selenium Grid will find the relevant node and route all the commands to be executed there. Follow these steps to write tests against the grid:

1. Create a new test file.

2. Populate the file with a test script that accesses an item on the grid and then works against `http://book.theautomatedtester.co.uk/`. Your script should look something like the following:

```
import org.junit.*;
import org.openqa.selenium.*;
import org.openqa.selenium.firefox.*;

import java.io.File;
import java.util.Dictionary;

public class TestExample1 {

  WebDriver driver;

  @Before
  public void setUp(){
    DesiredCapabilities capability =
      DesiredCapabilities.firefox();
    capability.setBrowserName("firefox" );
    // Set the platform we want our tests to run on
    capability.setPlatform("LINUX");
    driver = new RemoteWebDriver(new URL(
      "http://<grid hub>:4444/wd/hub"), capability);
```

```
    driver.get("http://book.theautomatedtester.co.uk/chapter1");
}

@After
public void tearDown(){
    driver.quit();
}

@Test
public void testExamples(){
    // We will put examples in here
}
```

We have just seen how we can write tests that can run against the grid and then run them. When the tests are running, the grid will show which browsers are currently in use and which grid items are currently free.

Running tests in parallel

So far we have managed to get our tests cycling through different machines. We also got it working against the Selenium Grid hub so that we can see all of our tests being split out to the machines and make sure that we test against browser and operating system combinations.

In this section, we will look at how we can add a thread-count attribute to the `<suite>` node in our test configuration file. We will also need to add the parallel attribute to the test suite. The value that it takes will either be methods or classes. This will mean that either the methods—the test cases—are run in parallel, or the classes that contain the test cases are running in parallel.

Getting our tests running in parallel

Now, we are ready to have our tests running in parallel:

1. Open your `TestNG` XML configuration file.
2. Add `parallel=methods` to the suite node.
3. Add `thread-count=3` to the suite node. This will run your tests with three threads. This number can be any value that you want. It is a best practice to know that the number of threads running is the number of cores that the machine is running the tests on minus the number of Selenium Remote Controls running.
4. Right-click on the configuration file in IDEA and run the tests.

We just managed to get our tests running in parallel. As you can see, this has been fairly easy. We saw that adding the parallel and the thread-count attributes allows us to run these tests in parallel and when coupled with Selenium Grid, we can start to get our tests running near *1/n*, which is where we want our tests to be.

Summary

We learned a lot in this chapter about how we can set up Selenium Grid and all the different arguments needed, as well as running our tests against the grid.

For more details, visit `https://code.google.com/p/selenium/wiki/Grid2`.

Specifically, we covered the following topics:

- **Starting the Selenium Grid Hub**: In this section of the book, we had a look at how we can start up the Selenium Grid Hub that is the central point for Selenium Grid.

- **Setting up Selenium Grid nodes**: We had a look at all the arguments that are needed to add a Selenium Server to the grid so that we can use it. This gives us a more manageable view of our grid so that we can work with it.

- **Running tests in parallel**: In this section, we learned how we can run our tests in parallel. We also had a look at how we can cycle through different browsers using the `@Parameter` annotation.

We also discussed how we can create tests that use the grid.

Now that we've learned about setting up Selenium Grid and looked into getting our test time down by running things in parallel using Selenium Grid, we should have a look at using Selenium to do more advanced user interactions—which is the topic of the next chapter.

Self-test questions

1. What is the command required to start the Hub?
2. What is the URL where one can see what is happening on the grid?
3. How do you specify the port the remote control is running on?
4. How do you specify which browser you would like the remote control to be registered with?

10
Advanced User Interactions

As we saw in the previous chapters, clicking and typing is quite straightforward with Selenium WebDriver. Find the element and then interact with it. Unfortunately, a lot of the modern web applications that are being created are a lot more than just typing and clicking. In this chapter, we will have a look at how we can drag and drop and move the mouse to specific places on a page.

In this chapter, we will learn the following topics:

- What is the Advanced User Interactions API?
- Building up a sequence of actions and performing them

So, let's get on with it.

You will need to have the currently released version of Firefox for this section of the book. You will also need to do this chapter on Microsoft Windows or a Linux distribution or Mac OS X. This is required so that we can do native interactions. Native interactions inject events into the browser just like if you were typing on a keyboard. Selenium WebDriver will use synthetic events by injecting events onto the page via JavaScript.

What is Advanced User Interactions API?

The **Advanced User Interactions API** is a new, more comprehensive API for describing actions a user can perform on a web page. Normally, we need to find elements and then send actions through them. If we need to perform complex tasks such as holding down *Ctrl* and clicking, then this may not work.

The Advanced User Interactions allows us to build these complex interactions with elements in a really nice API. The API relies on two key interfaces for the interactions to work—keyboard and mouse.

Keyboard

The keyboard interface allows keys to be pressed, held down, and released. It also allows for normal typing.

The methods available are:

- `void sendKeys(CharSequence... keysToSend)`: This is similar to the existing `sendKeys(...)` method.

- `void pressKey(Keys keyToPress)`: This sends a key press only, without releasing it. This should only be implemented for modifier keys (*Control*, *Alt*, and *Shift*).

- `void releaseKey(Keys keyToRelease)`: This releases a modifier key.

Mouse

The mouse interface allows for mouse clicks, double-clicks, and context clicks as well as moving the mouse to a specific point or to a specific element on the page.

The methods available are as follows:

- `void click(WebElement onElement)`: This is similar to the existing `click()` method

- `void doubleClick(WebElement onElement)`: This double-clicks an element

- `void mouseDown(WebElement onElement)`: This holds down the left mouse button on an element

- `void mouseUp(WebElement onElement)`: This releases the mouse button on an element

- `void mouseMove(WebElement toElement)`: This moves (from the current location) to another element

- `void mouseMove(WebElement toElement, long xOffset, long yOffset)`: This moves (from the current location) to new coordinates (x coordinates of `toElement` + `xOffset`, Y coordinates of `toElement` + `yOffset`)

- `void contextClick(WebElement onElement)`: This performs a context-click (right-click) on an element

These methods are useful to know but when working and creating a sequence, it is better to use the `Actions` chain generator and then call `perform` on that class.

The Actions class

The `Actions` class allows us to build a chain of actions that we would like to perform. This means that we can build up a nice sequence, for example, "Press *Shift* and type something and then release", or if we want to work with a select that allows multiple selects, we can press *Shift* and then do the necessary clicks.

We do this by creating an `Actions` object. We then need to chain some calls together:

```
// Create Actions object passing in a WebDriver object
Actions builder = new Actions(driver);

// Chain some calls together and call build
Action dragAndDrop = builder.clickAndHold(someElement)
   .moveToElement(otherElement)
   .release(otherElement)
   .build();

// Perform the actions
dragAndDrop.perform();
```

Drag and drop

We have seen that drag and drop is one of the main things that people want to do with web applications. This allows them to build task boards that allow other people to drag and drop between different states. You may have seen applications like this if you work in an **Agile environment**.

Let's try and create a basic drag and drop example using the little bit we already know of the `Actions` class.

Creating an Actions method chain for dragging and dropping

A lot of web applications these days allow users to drag and drop what they want and where they want on the page. This is really nice from a usability point of view, but from a testability point, it is a nightmare!

We can get around this with the `Actions` API.

1. Open up IntelliJ and create a new Selenium WebDriver project.
2. Create a new class and a new test with the following code:
    ```
    WebDriver driver = new FirefoxDriver();
    driver.get("http://www.theautomatedtester.co.uk/demo2.html");
    ```

```
WebElement someElement = driver.findElement
    (By.xpath("//div[contains(@class,'draggable')]"));

WebElement otherElement =
    driver.findElement(By.className("droppable"));

Actions builder = new Actions(driver);
Action dragAndDrop = builder.clickAndHold(someElement)
    .moveToElement(otherElement)
    .release(otherElement)
    .build();

dragAndDrop.perform();
```

3. Run the test. You should see the following screenshot first:

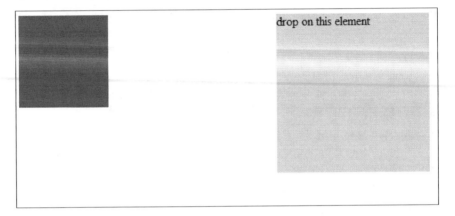

4. And when the test is complete, you will see the yellow block turn blue:

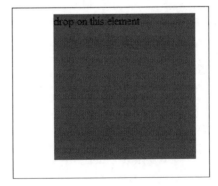

We have just seen how easy it is to do a drag and drop on the page. We just need to create an `Actions` class object and then create a chain of events. When we have built up the chain, we call `build()`. This puts everything in the right order and when we call `perform()`, the items are popped out of the queue and run in order.

Let's have a look at doing some slightly more complex chains with the `Actions` class.

Moving an element to an offset

We can get around this with the actions API. Here, we will learn how we can move the page object from one place to another on the browser.

Moving an element with a drag and drop by offset

There are times when we need to only move an image by a certain amount. A good example of this will be if you are working in a **WYSIWYG** editor and you wanted to just move an image to another place but did not want to drop it on another element, so you will be using `dragAndDropBy(WebElement, x, y);`.

Let's see this in action:

1. Open up IntelliJ and create a new Selenium WebDriver project.
2. Create a new class and a new test with the following code:

```
WebDriver driver = new FirefoxDriver();
driver.get("http://www.theautomatedtester.co.uk/demo2.html");
WebElement drag = driver.findElement(By.className("draggable"));

Actions builder = new Actions(driver);
  Action dragAndDrop = builder.dragAndDropBy(drag, 10, 20)
    .build();

dragAndDrop.perform();
```

3. Run the test. You should see the following screenshot:

We have just seen how easy it is to drag and drop on the page by moving an item by an offset. You will have to pass in the element that you want to move and then the x and y offset that you want to move it by.

The context click

If you are testing a highly rich application, such as a WYSIWYG editor or an e-mail client, you will more than likely need to do a context click or right-click to get other menu items. This may seem like a simple task as a user, but doing this within a browser and doing it programmatically has been a difficult task for some time. The interactions API allows us to do this and do it in a meaningful way.

We will now see it in action.

Doing a context click

If you are working in a document editor online or in an e-mail client and you are required to load a context menu, this will be useful. This can also be useful to load other bits of functionality or access specific pages.

To do this, we will have to do the following:

1. Open up IntelliJ and create a new Selenium WebDriver project.

2. Create a new class and a new test with the following code:

```
WebDriver driver = new FirefoxDriver();
driver.get("http://www.theautomatedtester.co.uk/demo1.html");
Actions builder = new Actions(driver);
```

```
WebElement element = driver.findElement(By.tagName("body"));
Action contextClick = builder.contextClick(element)
    .build();

contextClick.perform();
```

3. Run the test. You should see the following screenshot:

We managed to get our code to cause a right-click to happen on the page. This means that we can now get to areas of our application that have overridden the default behavior. We see this happening in a lot of WYSIWYG editors and in really rich HTML web applications.

Clicking on multiple items in a select element

When filling in forms, one of the nicest and quickest way to get information is to have a select that allows you to choose a number of items in the selection. Unfortunately, from a testing point of view, this can be really hard to do since each click will just select a new item instead of keeping the last one.

Selecting multiple items on a select item

A number of forms nowadays ask users to select a number of items from a list. For me, a good example is the **Advanced Search** option on **Bugzilla**. You can see an example at `https://bugzilla.mozilla.org/query.cgi?format=advanced`. In Selenium RC, selecting multiple items was impossible. Using the standard clicking and typing with Selenium WebDriver, we will not be able to do this either; however, we can get around this with these actions in the API:

1. Open up IntelliJ and create a new Selenium WebDriver project.

2. Create a new class and a new test with the following code:

```
WebDriver driver = new FirefoxDriver();
driver.get("http://book.theautomatedtester.co.uk/
multi-select.html");
Actions builder = new Actions(driver);

WebElement select = driver.findElement(By.xpath("//select[2]"));
List<WebElement> options = select.findElements(
   By.tagName("option"));
Action multipleSelect = builder.keyDown(Keys.SHIFT)
  .click(options.get(0))
  .click(options.get(2))
  .build();

multipleSelect.perform();
```

3. Run the test. You should see the following:

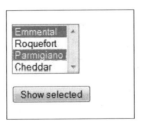

We have successfully done a multi-select. This can be useful for testing forms that allow users to select multiple items. The same principle can be used if you need to interact with anything that requires both the keyboard and the mouse to be used at the same time.

Clicking and holding down the mouse

Canvas applications are becoming one of the most used HTML5 components to be added to applications. One of the nice things that we can do with them is draw pictures on the page by just clicking and holding down the mouse.

From the automation point of view, this will appear to be extremely difficult. We have commands such as `click()` and we know that we can move an element by a specific offset, but a `click()` action doesn't do what we do.

Holding the mouse button down while moving the mouse

In this section, we will have a look at how we can press down the left mouse button and then move it around the page. If you are working on a canvas that tracks the mouse movements, you will be able to draw a picture with the actions API. Let's see this in action:

1. Open up IntelliJ and create a new Selenium WebDriver project.
2. Create a new class and a new test with the following code:

```
WebDriver driver = new FirefoxDriver();
driver.get('http://www.theautomatedtester.co.uk/demo1.html')

Actions builder = new Actions(driver);
WebElement canvas = driver.findElement(By.id("tutorial"));
Action dragAndDrop = builder.clickAndHold(canvas)
  .moveByOffset(-40, -60)
  .moveByOffset(20, 20)
  .moveByOffset(100, 150)
  .release(canvas)
  .build();

dragAndDrop.perform();
```

3. Run the test. You should see the following screenshot:

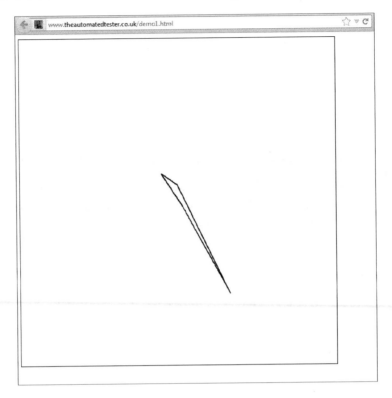

We just saw how easy it is to hold the mouse button down and move it all over the page and then release the buttons. This type of action is one of the most complex types of work that we will have to do since it joins together a few different actions.

Summary

We learned a lot in this chapter about using the Advanced User Interactions API. We saw how we can use it to work against web applications that have a large amount of key strokes or complex mouse movements.

Specifically, we covered the following topics:

- **What is the Advanced User API**: In this section, we learned what the API is and what makes it up. This is important since it sets us up for understanding the rest of the chapter.

- **The Actions class**: In this section, we saw how we can start using the action chains to start building up complex chains of interactions with the page from typing to mouse movements. One thing to note is that the mouse won't appear to move but the right events will fire.

Now that we've learned about Advanced User Interactions, we have finished learning all of the core aspects of Selenium. Now, we can learn about good design patterns for writing tests—which is the topic of the next chapter.

Self-test questions

1. Which is the class that contains the action chain generator?
2. Which is the method that builds up the chain?
3. Which is the method that executes the chain in the order that it is created?
4. Which is the best way to move the mouse by x coordinates to the side and Y coordinates up?

11
Working with HTML5

HTML5 has become one of the latest buzzwords to hit web development in the last couple of years. It has brought a number of useful items to web developers that make web applications act more like desktop applications. In this chapter, we will have a look at a number of the different technologies that cannot be accessed by normal clicking or typing.

In this chapter, we will learn the following topics:

- Application cache
- Browser connections
- Web storage

So, let's get on with it.

This only works with `AndroidDriver`, `IPhoneDriver`, though some of it works in Firefox. When working through the examples, we will need to make sure that we use those objects. We will use the example class, as follows:

```
importorg.junit.*;
importorg.openqa.selenium.*;

public class TestChapter10 {

  WebDriver driver;

  @Before
  public void setUp(){
    driver = new AndroidDriver();
    driver.get("http://book.theautomatedtester.co.uk/chapter4");
  }
```

```
@After
public void tearDown(){
  driver.quit();
}

@Test
public void testExamples(){
  // We will put examples in here
}
}
```

Working with application cache

The application cache is one of the new features of HTML5. It allows web applications to specify the files that are downloaded when the browser accesses the page. The browser looks at the files in the application cache before opening any network connections to the server. This means that if the computer or mobile device goes offline, then those files are still available and loaded straightaway.

To see if your application has an application cache file, you need to have a look at the source of the HTML document. It should have a manifest attribute in the HTML tag as follows:

```
<html manifest="example.appcache">
...
</html>
```

When items are downloaded, we can then make calls to the application cache object that is attached to the window object in the browser.

Selenium WebDriver has AppCacheStatusenum that represents the current status of the application cache. The status are as follows:

- **0**: UNCACHED
- **1**: IDLE
- **2**: CHECKING
- **3**: DOWNLOADING
- **4**: UPDATEREADY
- **5**: OBSOLETE

Let's try using them.

Getting the current status of application cache

One of the things that you want to do during testing is to make sure that the application cache is storing your files. We can see if they have been downloaded. Refer to the following steps:

1. Create a new test class using the example code at the beginning of the chapter.

2. In this part, we are just going to check if the application cache is working. We do this with the following piece of code:

```
AppCacheStatus status = (ApplicationCache) driver).getStatus();
```

3. The status should be equal to uncached when we load it.

4. The final class should look like the following:

```
importorg.junit.*;
importorg.openqa.selenium.*;

public class TestChapter10 {

  WebDriver driver;

  @Before
  public void setUp(){
    driver = new AndroidDriver();
    driver.get("http://book.theautomatedtester.co.uk/");
  }

  @After
  public void tearDown(){
    driver.quit();
  }

  @Test
  public void testAppCacheStatus(){
    AppCacheStatus status = (ApplicationCache)
    driver).getStatus();
    assertEqual(status AppCacheStatus.UNCACHED);
  }
}
```

We just saw how we can get the application cache from the browser using the API built into Selenium WebDriver. We will get an enum returned that relates to the current status that the browser returns. Now we know that we have the means to have a look at how our web application will act if it were to go offline.

Interacting with browser connections

Now that we can download and cache files using the application cache, it will be a good idea to see how well they work when there is no network connection. The mobile drivers have the ability to go into airplane mode. Hopefully, future versions of desktop browsers will have this ability too.

We will start by having a look at whether the browser is online.

Seeing if the browser is online

Seeing if a browser is online during a test can be quite useful when we are testing how our application works offline. This is useful for working against sites that have the application cache configured so you can check whether the site works when offline. We first need to make sure we know how to check if the browser is online.

Let's see how this looks.

Checking the browser status

In this section, we will have a look at whether the browser is online or offline. Currently, this only works on mobile drivers from Selenium WebDriver. In this section, we will need to cast the Selenium WebDriver object to BrowserConnection and then access the methods that are found on that object.

Let's get into action:

1. Create a new test class using the example code at the beginning of the chapter. We can call the TestBrowserConnection class.

2. Create a test method and add the following to it:

   ```
   assertTrue(((BrowserConnection) driver).isOnline());
   ```

3. Your class should look like the following and when you run the test method, it will pass:

   ```
   importorg.junit.*;
   importorg.openqa.selenium.*;
   ```

```
public class TestChapter10 {

  WebDriver driver;

  @Before
  public void setUp(){
    driver = new AndroidDriver();
    driver.get("http://book.theautomatedtester.co.uk/");
  }

  @After
  public void tearDown(){
    driver.quit();
  }

  @Test
  public void testBrowserConnection(){
    assertTrue(((BrowserConnection) driver).isOnline());
  }
}
```

We have seen that, by casting the `webdriver` object to `BrowserConnection`, we have access to a number of new methods. These methods allow us to see if the browser is currently online or offline. They also allow us to set the browser to online or offline, which is the next section of this book.

Setting the browser offline or online

Now that we know how to see if the browser is online or offline, let's have a look at setting the browser connection to online or offline. This is not part of HTML5, but will allow us to use the previous online call, which is part of HTML5, and to check if our application cache has downloaded the relevant files.

Let's see this in action.

Setting the browser connection

In this section, we will turn the device's browser connectivity off. This means that we can check how the application works if it were offline. This will be a really useful feature as more and more applications take advantage of the move to mobile.

Let's see this in action:

1. We will create a new test method in the class that we created in the previous section.

2. In the test, we need to set the browser offline. We do this by casting to `BrowserConnection` and then using the `setOnline()` method. If we pass in `true`, it will set it online and if we set it to `false`, it will set the browser offline. The following is an example:

   ```
   ((BrowserConnection) driver).setOnline(false);
   ```

3. When you have finished, your class should look like the following:

   ```java
   importorg.junit.*;
   importorg.openqa.selenium.*;

   public class TestChapter10 {

       WebDriver driver;

       @Before
       public void setUp(){
           driver = new AndroidDriver();
           driver.get("http://book.theautomatedtester.co.uk/");
       }

       @After
       public void tearDown(){
           driver.quit();
       }

       @Test
       public void testBrowserConnectionOnline(){
           assertTrue(((BrowserConnection) driver).isOnline());
       }

       @Test
       Public void testTurnOffConnectivity(){
           BrowserConnectionnetworkAwareDriver = (BrowserConnection)
           driver;
           networkAwareDriver.setOnline(false);
           assertFalse(networkAwareDriver.isOnline());
           networkAwareDriver.setOnline(true);
           assertFalse(networkAwareDriver.isOnline());


       }
   }
   ```

We saw that we can simply turn the browser connection on and off on these devices and check that the browser is in the correct state, either online or offline, before moving on with the test.

Now we will move on to how to access some HTML5 storage technologies.

Working with WebStorage

Some of the other technologies that are being developed for HTML5 are related to WebStorage. There are three main WebStorage technologies:

- Local storage
- Session storage
- WebSQL

In this section of the chapter, we will only be working with the first two since WebSQL is not being implemented by all of the browser vendors. These technologies allow us to save to the users' hard disk and then retrieve what we stored.

Local storage

In this section, we will have a look at local storage to make sure that items we expect to be there are really there. This is analogous to an integration test that accesses a database to check whether something has been sorted. LocalStorage allows data to be stored and the data is persisted between sessions the browser is closed and reopened.

The Selenium WebDriver object called LocalStorage is used to access the local storage in the browser. The API is nearly a 1:1 match for the JavaScript API that comes with browsers.

Let's see this in action.

Accessing localStorage

Imagine that your application has stored something in localStorage while the user was interacting with the application. An example of this might be working in a word processing application and it auto saving every so often. If your application were offline, it can still save the information.

Let's see how we access this:

1. Create a new test class. You can use the example code at the beginning of the chapter to help you create it quicker.

2. Accessing the `LocalStorage` object will require us to case the `WebDriver` object to it. This is similar to what we saw with `BrowserConnection` previously.

```
LocalStoragestorageDriver = (LocalStorage) driver;
storageDriver.size(); // returns 0 if there is nothing in there
```

3. Now run your test class. It should look something like the following:

```
importorg.junit.*;
importorg.openqa.selenium.*;

public class TestChapter10 {

    WebDriver driver;

    @Before
    public void setUp(){
        driver = new AndroidDriver();
        driver.get("http://book.theautomatedtester.co.uk/
        localStorage.html");
    }

    @After
    public void tearDown(){
        driver.quit();
    }

    @Test
    public void testShouldReturnCurrentLocalStorageSize(){
        assertEqual(0, ((LocalStorage) driver).size();
    }
}
```

We just saw how we can access `LocalStorage`, the Selenium WebDriver API, to access the browsers' `localStorage` object. This means that we can have a look and check what the application has stored on the user's local storage.

Session storage

Session storage is a technology very similar to local storage. The main difference is that it does not persist. If you were to close the tab and then reopen it while using Firefox, for example, session storage items will not be available while local storage will still be available.

Let's see how we can work with it.

Accessing sessionStorage

Imagine again that you are working against a word processing application but, instead of it auto saving the text that you type to somewhere that is persisted, you only save it briefly, waiting for the user to click save.

Let us see how we can use it.

1. Let's just add a new `testMethod` to the class we created in the previous section. We can call it `testShouldAccessSessionStorage()`.

2. We will need to cast the `WebDriver` object to a `SessionStorage` object, so we can start accessing the methods it has available, like the following:

    ```
    SessionStorage storage = (SessionStorage) driver;
    assertEquals(0, storage.size());
    ```

3. Let's create our test and run it. It should look like the following:

    ```
    importorg.junit.*;
    importorg.openqa.selenium.*;

    public class TestChapter10 {

      WebDriver driver;

      @Before
      public void setUp(){
        driver = new AndroidDriver();
        driver.get("http://book.theautomatedtester.co.uk/
        localStorage.html");
      }

      @After
      public void tearDown(){
        driver.quit();
      }
    ```

```
@Test
public void testShouldReturnCurrentLocalStorageSize(){
  assertEqual(0, ((SessionStorage) driver).size();
}
}
```

We just saw that the `SessionStorage` object acts a lot like the `localStorage` object that we worked with in the previous section of the chapter. We were able to get the `SessionStorage` methods by casting the Selenium `WebDriver` object. This gives us access to methods that map over to the JavaScript API available in the browser.

Summary

We learned a lot in this chapter about using the HTML5 API that comes with Selenium WebDriver. These are helper methods that make our lives significantly easier when working against application cache or against web storage mechanisms.

Specifically, we covered:

- **The application cache API**: We had a look at how we can access the browsers' application cache to see if it is downloading items into the cache or if the current app is uncached.

- **Browser connections**: Web applications, with the help of HTML5, are getting the ability to work when they are offline. We have seen how, with the help of the application cache, we can load pages from the cache. We can also see whether the browser is currently online or offline, and on the mobile devices we can turn them to airplane mode.

- **WebStorage**: In this section, we had a look at how we can access the `WebStorage` object that has been added to the HTML5 specification. Specifically, we had a look at `localStorage` and `sessionStorage`. Selenium WebDriver has tried to emulate the APIs available in the browser in the Selenium WebDriver APIs.

 If you want to read more on session storage, I recommend that you read `https://developer.mozilla.org/en-US/docs/DOM/Storage#sessionStorage`.

Now that we've learned about working with HTML5, we're ready to work through the final advanced topics—which is the topic of the next chapter.

Self-test questions

1. Which one of the following is a Web Storage features?

    a. Local storage

    b. Session storage

    c. Both a and b

    d. None of the above

2. Which one of the following is `AppCacheStatusenum` that represents the current status of the application cache is correct?

    a. 0: UNCACHED

    b. 1: CHECKING

    c. 2: IDLE

    d. All are wrong

12
Advanced Topics

In this chapter, we will have a look at a number of advanced topics associated with Selenium WebDriver. These are not required to use Selenium WebDriver, but will be useful when there will be problems with testing.

In this chapter, we will learn the following topics:

- Capturing screenshots
- Using XVFB with Selenium
- Working with Browsermob Proxy

So, let's get on with it.

Before we start, it will be good to download all the necessary items. Download the latest version from Browsermob Proxy: `https://github.com/webmetrics/browsermob-proxy/downloads`, and for XVFB, select `sudo apt-get install xvfb`.

XVFB only works reliably on Linux. Unfortunately, this will not work on Windows. The following is a screenshot displaying the information to install `sudo apt-get install xvfb`:

```
davidburns@ubuntu:~$ sudo apt-get install xvfb
Reading package lists... Done
Building dependency tree
Reading state information... Done
The following NEW packages will be installed:
  xvfb
0 upgraded, 1 newly installed, 0 to remove and 0 not upgraded.
Need to get 866 kB of archives.
After this operation, 2,068 kB of additional disk space will be used.
Get:1 http://us.archive.ubuntu.com/ubuntu/ oneiric-updates/main xvfb amd64 2:1.10.4-1ubuntu4.2 [866 kB]
Fetched 866 kB in 3s (230 kB/s)
Selecting previously deselected package xvfb.
(Reading database ... 228914 files and directories currently installed.)
Unpacking xvfb (from .../xvfb_2%3a1.10.4-1ubuntu4.2_amd64.deb) ...
Processing triggers for man-db ...
Setting up xvfb (2:1.10.4-1ubuntu4.2) ...
davidburns@ubuntu:~$
```

Capturing screenshots

A lot of times, our Selenium remote control browsers run on different machines than the machine that performs tests. This is because you, as a developer or tester, need a mechanism to have a screenshot of what an error looks like when the test fails. The screenshots that are captured are saved in the PNG format.

Unfortunately, capturing screenshots in Selenium is limited to popular browsers such as Mozilla Firefox, Google Chrome, and Internet Explorer. This is because these browsers have libraries that Selenium can use to take screenshots. As more libraries are added to Selenium for different browsers, you will be able to take more screenshots. They will use the same API call so that there will be no need to change your tests.

The screenshot's capability lives within an interface called `TakesScreenshot`. We will cast the driver to this and then use the interface to access the `getScreenshotAs()` method. You also need to import the following library:

```
import static openqa.selenium.OutputType.*;
```

Capturing the base64 version of images

In this section, we will have a look at capturing a base64 representation of a screenshot. Base64 is a group of encoding schemes that allow us to represent binary data as ASCII. A common use for them in web applications is to place data URLs as the source for images to save on downloads that the browser has to do when it is parsing the HTML.

Image capturing as base64 strings

Imagine that you want to take a screenshot on Selenium Grid. When you take the screenshot, you don't want it to be saved to the hard drive of the Selenium Grid node. You want it to be moved back to where your tests are, especially if you are using it with a Continuous Integration box. Refer to the following steps to take screenshots as base64 strings:

1. Open up Eclipse and create a new Java test class.

2. Add a new line to take a screenshot:

   ```
   driver.get(http://book.theautomatedtester.co.uk);
   String screenshotBase64 = ((Screenshot)
     driver).getScreenshotAs(base64);
   ```

3. If you set a breakpoint on the previous line, you will be able to see what the string looks like.

We have just managed to take a screenshot and have it returned as a base64 string. This will allow us to take a screenshot on a remote machine and then transport the resulting image back to where the test is being run from.

Saving the screenshot to bytes

Now that we have had a look at capturing screenshots to base64 strings, let's have a look at capturing them as bytes. Having them as bytes means that we can transform them into a number of different things.

Saving images to bytes

Imagine that you want to do some in-depth analysis of the UI by taking screenshots. This is something that has been done a number of times in different projects. For example, you take a screenshot, then make changes, and then take more screenshots along the way. Refer to the following steps to save images into bytes:

1. Open up IntelliJ and create a new Java test class.

2. Add a new line to take a screenshot:

    ```
    driver.get(http://book.theautomatedtester.co.uk);
    Bytes screenbytes = ((Screenshot)driver).getScreenshotAs(bytes);
    ```

3. If you set a breakpoint on the previous line, you will be able to see what the string looks like.

Now that we have seen what it takes to take a screenshot of the page from the browser, we have managed to take a screenshot and pushed the result into a `bytes` variable. We can then perform histogram type checks against the bytes and anything else that we want.

We can also push the bytes into a stream to save it to a file or we can take screenshots straight to files.

Saving screenshots to file is probably the most common way to save a file. This approach will save the file to disk straightaway. When we save the screenshot as a file, we are returned a `file` object.

We can then use it straightaway to do anything like `getPath()` or do what we need.

Saving a screenshot to file

In this section, we will have a look at how we can save a file to disk. This is the most common thing that people do when saving screenshots. One thing to note is that if you are using Remote WebDriver, this will save the file on the same machine as the Selenium Server. Refer to the following steps to save a screenshot to a file:

1. Open up Eclipse and create a new Java test class.

2. Add a new line to take a screenshot:

   ```
   driver.get(http://book.theautomatedtester.co.uk);
   File savedImage = ((Screenshot)driver).getScreenshotAs(file);
   ```

3. If you set a breakpoint on the previous line, you will be able to see what the string looks like.

We have just seen what is the most common way to save screenshots. When we take the screenshot, the image is saved to the disk and we are returned the `file` object that has access to that image.

If you'd like to move the file it is created, you can use the following code snippet:

```
File imageFile = ((TakesScreenshot) driver)
  .getScreenshotAs(OutputType.FILE);
String failureImageFileName = "testfailureimage.png";

File failureImageFile = new File(failureImageFileName);
FileUtils.moveFile(imageFile, failureImageFile);
```

Using XVFB with Selenium

The following section of this book requires work in Linux as the requirements are only available on this platform. When Selenium is running on your machine, you will see that it always runs on your screen. If you want to push the running of your tests to the background, you need to use XVFB (**X11 Virtual Frame Buffer**).

This allows us to run tests with a browser without it trying to steal focus from you. FirefoxDriver, for example, forces the browser to the foreground to help native events.

Setting up XVFB server

We will have to make sure that we have XVFB running on our machine. This should be fairly easy to get it right. Refer to the following steps to set up an XVFB server:

1. Open a terminal.

2. In the terminal, run the following command:

   ```
   Xvfb :1 -screen 0 1600x1200x32
   ```

3. The server will listen for connections as the server number, 1, and screen, 0, has a depth of 32 1600x1200.

4. You should see something like the following screenshot on your terminal:

```
davidburns@ubuntu:~$ Xvfb :2 -screen 1 1600x1200x16
[dix] Could not init font path element /usr/share/fonts/X11/cyrillic, removing f
rom list!
[dix] Could not init font path element /usr/share/fonts/X11/100dpi/:unscaled, re
moving from list!
[dix] Could not init font path element /usr/share/fonts/X11/75dpi/:unscaled, rem
oving from list!
[dix] Could not init font path element /usr/share/fonts/X11/100dpi, removing fro
m list!
[dix] Could not init font path element /usr/share/fonts/X11/75dpi, removing from
list!
```

We have just seen what it takes to set up XVFB on our machines. We have just told it to start an XVFB server and set up a screen on that server. If you want to set up XVFB in different ways, I recommend that you read the manual at http://www.xfree86.org/4.0.1/Xvfb.1.html.

Running tests in XVFB

Now that we have the server up and running, we can have a look at making sure that when we run our tests, they will use the new display.

We will have to make sure that we have XVFB running on the machine:

1. Open the terminal.

2. We need to export the display so that everything that is launched from it uses the one that we have set up earlier. We do this with the following command:

   ```
   Export DISPLAY=0.1
   ```

3. Now we just need to run our tests. You will see that the browser may launch in the dock, but it should not actually be visible.

We have successfully managed to get our tests running using XVFB. We saw that the tests that we were running, and launching a browser on our displays, still finished with the same results.

This is useful in situations you have your tests running on change and you know that the browser will not try stealing focus.

 Now that we know how to run tests with XVFB, try to run with tests in parallel and see how this works!

Working with BrowserMob Proxy

Patrick Lightbody, one of the core originators of Selenium and the creator of Selenium RC with Paul Hammant, created the BrowserMob proxy while working on his start-up, BrowserMob. BrowserMob Proxy allows you to control the way traffic is filtered to the browser.

We can also change the headers that are supplied to the server. This allows us to do a number of things.

Creating and starting a proxy

When working with BrowserMob Proxy, we will need to make sure that we start the proxy so that we can use the API and change what we need.

We will need to start the proxy and make sure that we can then interact with it:

1. Create a new Project in IntelliJ.

2. Add the BrowserMob JAR files to the project so that we can use it:

```
ProxyServer proxy = New ProxyServer(9876);
proxy.start();
```

3. When we want to stop the server, we just call the following method:

```
proxy.stop()
```

We successfully started the server by passing in the port. The server needs to be started before we can do any of the different tasks that we will be doing in the future sections of the book.

Capturing network traffic

One of the most useful things in Selenium Remote Control is the ability to capture the network traffic of the application that you are testing. To capture network traffic, we need to proxy all traffic through BrowserMob Proxy. The way that BrowserMob Proxy does this is by capturing the network traffic and pushing it into a format called **HTTP Archive** or most commonly known as **HAR**. A HAR file is in JSON format, which is the standard way to represent network traffic.

HAR captures a lot of information that can be used for different purposes, so we will learn how to capture it next.

Imagine that you wanted to see whether there was anything on the page that was not found. This can be images, CSS files, or JavaScript files. These things are not visible when working on a page, and it can be interesting with unexpected bugs. We will now see how we can create a HAR file and then capture it.

Since the HAR will return the JSON we need, we just need to parse the JSON format returned to get what we want:

1. Using the project we created previously, we add a few more lines to get what we want.

2. We need to tell Selenium WebDriver that we have a proxy that it has to use. We can do that with the following lines of code:

```
FirefoxProfile profile = new FirefoxProfile();
profile.setProxy(proxy.seleniumProxy);
```

3. We need to tell the proxy to create a new HAR file for us. We will do this by adding the following line:

```
Proxy.newHar("PageName"); // PageName is the name of the page we
want to capture
```

4. We then need to load a page, we do this by clicking on a link called the `get()` link.

5. Now, we need to call `proxy.getHar()`.This will return the HAR that we wanted.

6. Your code should look like the folllowing:

```
FirefoxProfile profile = new FirefoxProfile();
profile.setProxy(proxy.seleniumProxy);
WebDriver driver = new FirefoxDriver(profile);
proxy.newHar("PageName");
driver.get("http://book.theautomatedtester.co.uk
proxy.getHar();
```

7. Also your HAR, once put through a JSON viewer should look like the following screenshot:

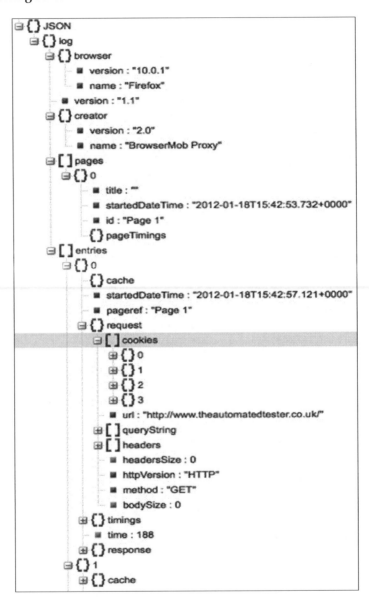

We have just captured the network traffic while running our tests. This can be really useful if you want to check weather there are any `404` responses when loading our application under test. This can be useful if you are moving things about or if you are doing a smoke test after you have deployed your application to production.

Now that we have managed to get the proxy started and managed to record the network traffic, which is going through to the browser, try to get the proxy to slow down the time that a response takes to get through. BrowserMob Proxy supports this and IntelliJ can help with what parts of the API to use.

Summary

We learned a lot in this chapter about some of the advanced topics that we may need in tougher times!

Specifically, we covered the following topics:

- **Saving screenshots**: You learned how to save screenshots of our web applications programmatically. This allows you to know when something happens, and you need to see what caused it!

- **Using XVFB**: In this section, you learned how to use XVFB to have a virtual display to run our tests in. This can be really useful if you want to run Selenium WebDriver and not worry that when tests run, the browser might suddenly steal focus. This is useful if you are running a number of tests on a single machine and they need to use native events that Selenium WebDriver tries to do on Windows and Linux.

- **BrowserMob Proxy**: In this section, we had a look at how we can replicate Selenium Remote Control's `captureNetworkTraffic()` method that allows us to see what the browser downloaded during a page load. This is useful if you are doing web performance analysis during tests.

We should also note that BrowserMob Proxy can do a lot more than record network traffic. It can block content from certain URLs, such as ad networks, which can improve the speed at which tests run. This might be something to consider if your tests take hours and it is tracked down to a web performance issue.

Now that we've learned about these topics, you should feel confident about using Selenium WebDriver and testing it against a number of the different web applications out there!

Self-test questions

1. What is the easiest approach to saving images?

    a. Base64 string

    b. Bytes

    c. File

2. If you want to move a screenshot over Selenium Grid, which is the best output type to choose?

3. What does XVFB stand for?

4. What argument do we need to pass in when starting XVFB to have it start up on a specific display?

5. What is the name of the JSON format for showing network traffic?

6. What is the call that tells BrowserMob Proxy to start recording traffic?

13
Migrating from Remote Control to WebDriver

Selenium Remote Control has been around for a number of years. This means that there is a large amount of tests out there written for the API. If you ever have to migrate your test suite, then this chapter will give you the insight that you need.

In this chapter, we will cover the WebDriverBackedSelenium object.

Before we work through this chapter, it might be a good idea to go through *Chapter 4*, *Finding Elements*, again as this will minimize the amount of work that is required as we move to WebDriver.

So, let's get on with it.

WebDriverBackedSelenium

Unfortunately, we spent a considerable time in the past few years developing Selenium Remote Control tests, and converting them over to the new style of Selenium WebDriver might not be feasible. The WebDriver API is fundamentally different in its design compared to Selenium RC.

With this in mind, the Selenium Core development team has created the WebDriverBackedSelenium object that we can use. This allows us to create our tests with Selenium Remote Control syntax that we already know but have some of the benefits of WebDriver with a very minor change to what you currently have. Refer to the following code example:

```
String baseUrl = "http://book.theautomatedtester.co.uk";
String remoteControl = "localhost";
Int port = 4444;
String browser = "*firefox";
```

```
Selenium selenium = new DefaultSelenium(remoteControl, port ,
   browser ,baseUrl);
selenium.start();
selenium.open("/");
selenium.click("link=chapter1");
// rest of the test code
```

We then need to change our tests to the following:

```
WebDriver driver = new FirefoxDriver();
String baseUrl = "http://book.theautomatedtester.co.uk";
Selenium selenium = new WebDriverBackedSelenium(driver,baseUrl);
selenium.open("/");
selenium.click("link=chapter1");
// rest of the test code
```

Let's try to convert one of our Selenium Remote Control tests.

Converting tests to Selenium WebDriver using WebDriverBackedSelenium

Let's take one of our Selenium Remote Control tests and change it to use
`WebDriverBackedSelenium`. This should be a simple change. Refer to
the following code and then follow the steps:

```
import com.thoughtworks.selenium.*;
import org.junit.*;

public class TestSeleniumWebDriver {
   // We can name this file what we want

   Selenium selenium;

   @Before
   public void setup(){
      selenium = new DefaultSelenium("localhost",4444,"*chrome",
         "http://book.theautomatedtester.co.uk");
      selenium.start();
   }

   @Test
   public void shouldOpenChapter2LinkAndVerifyAButton(){
```

```
    /* This will contain some actions for us. We are going
     * to be concentrating on the @Before and @After methods
    }


  @After
  public void teardown(){
    selenium.stop();
  }
}
```

1. Open IDEA or Eclipse and load your example.

2. Create a new external library for the Selenium binaries. We learned how to do this in *Chapter 3, Overview of the Selenium WebDriver.*

3. Add the variable WebDriver driver at the top of your class.

4. Change your setup() to look like the following:

```
@Before
public void setup(){
  driver = new FirefoxDriver();
  selenium = new WebDriverBackedSelenium(driver,
    http://book.theautomatedtester.co.uk)
}
```

5. Change the teardown() to the following code:

```
@After
public void teardown(){
  driver.quit();
}
```

6. Run your tests.

We have seen how, with very little change to our tests, we got our old Selenium Remote Control tests working using the new Selenium WebDriver drivers. The WebDriverBackedSelenium object has a mapping of the Selenium Remote Control API to the Selenium WebDriver API.

When the browser starts, you will see the WebDriver extension in the bottom right of the browser. When it is processing commands, it will turn red, and when it isn't, it will be black. It should look like the following screenshots:

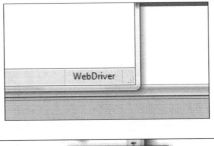

There are a few items that are not fully supported by WebDriverBackedSelenium, but hopefully, as more and more work is done to the framework, these will be less noticeable. This is available to all languages that can communicate with the remote server.

Summary

We saw that we can easily move from tests that we created in the past using the Selenium Remote Control API.

Specifically, we covered the following topics:

- **Switching to WebDriverBackedSelenium**: In this section, we saw that with only a few lines changed within our tests, we can suddenly be running with Selenium WebDriver, the new API in the Selenium project. This not only allows us to fully migrate our tests but also gives us a starting point. Remember that WebDriverBackedSelenium can work in all languages. You can either use the object or inject a WebDriver Object into the Selenium Object and have the Selenium Server do all of the work for you.

Self-test question

1. How do you use WebDriverBackedSelenium?

A
Automation Prerequisites for Selenium Automation

Considering we use Java as a programming language used for Selenium automation, in this chapter, we will learn prerequisites required for Selenium automation. We will have to look at the basics of core Java, which is very much required for Selenium WebDriver. And also, we will learn to understand a few object-oriented concepts taking Java as a programming language.

At the end of this chapter, we will be in a position to write basic programs using core Java and will be able to understand the OOPs concepts as well, where we can use the concepts and basic programming while doing Selenium automation.

About Java programming

Java is a general-purpose computer programming language that is concurrent, class-based, and object-oriented. It includes the following functionalities:

- Real-world programming
- Reusability (reuse of components once created)
- Modularity (modifying a required object without affecting the functionality of the other object)
- Resilience to change (redefining the system without any major change in other parts)
- Information hiding (limited access to information can be given to the user, resulting in security in a program)

How does Java work?

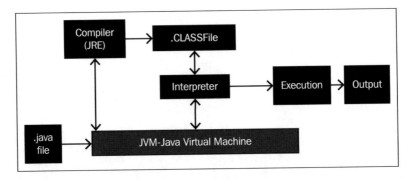

1. Java programs are written in .java files.

2. When the .java file is executed, Java Virtual Machine (JVM) will interact with one of its components, Compiler, which will convert the .java file to a .class file.

3. Interpreter is another component of Java Virtual Machine that will interact with the .class file in runtime, that is, at the time of execution, and this provides the output.

[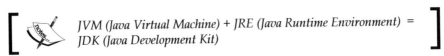 *JVM (Java Virtual Machine) + JRE (Java Runtime Environment) = JDK (Java Development Kit)*]

Package

A package is a collection of classes and interfaces that provides a high-level layer of access protection and namespace management.

At a high level, its a folder where the Java classes are placed.

Class

A class defines the structure and behavior of an object or set of objects.

Objects

Objects are the basic building blocks of the OOP, and they can also be defined as an instance of a class.

Objects have the following characteristics:

- State: The state of an object is indicated by a set of attributes and the values of these attributes.

- Behavior: The behavior of an object refers to the change of its state over a period of time.

- Identity: Each object has a unique identity for identification.

- A class in the object-oriented methodology is a collection of various attributes, such as data and methods. You can access the data of a class using its methods.

 The Main method is the entry point of execution in a Java program.

Importing the sample Java project in the Eclipse workspace

The following are the steps to run the sample programs:

1. Launch Eclipse.
2. Import the project (**File | Import | Existing Project | Java project path**) `MySampleJavaProject` as an existing project.
3. Enable the **Navigator** view on Eclipse (from **Window Tab | Show View**).
4. Right-click on the `.java` file and select **Run as Java Application**.

A simple Java program example

The following is an example of a Java program:

```
package pckg1;
public class example1 {
  public static void main(String[] args) {
    // TODO Auto-generated method stub
    System.out.println("I am done with my 1st program on java");
  }
}
```

The output for the preceding code will be as follows:

```
I am done with my 1st program on java
```

Inheritance

Inheritance enables you to extend the functionality of an existing class.

In inheritance, a superclass or a parent class is the one from which another class inherits attributes and behavior. A subclass or **child class** is a class that inherits attributes and behavior from a superclass.

 Th object class is called as a supermost class. Inheritance is applicable only for nonstatic classes.

A Java program with an inheritance example

The following is an example of inheritance in a Java program:

```java
package MyFirstPackage;

class SampleClass1 {
  void sampleMethod(){
  System.out.println("executing sample method");
}
 }

class SampleClass2 extends SampleClass1 {
    void sampleMethod1(){
    System.out.println("executing sample method 2");
  }
  }


public  class Inhertance {
  public static void main(String[] args) {
    SampleClass2 methodcall = new SampleClass2();
    methodcall.sampleMethod1();
    methodcall.sampleMethod();
  }
}
```

The output of the preceding code will be as follows:

executing sample method 2

executing sample method

An abstract class

An abstract class is a class that has one or more methods with no definitions or body. This class must be inherited and must be a superclass and obviously a nonstatic class.

An example of a Java program with an abstract class

The following is an example of an abstract class in a Java program:

```
package MyFirstPackage;

abstract  class sample_abs {

  abstract void abstr_method ();
  abstract void abstr_method1 ();
  abstract void abstr_method2 ();
  abstract void abstr_method3 ();
  abstract void abstr_method4 ();

  void nonabstr (){
  }
}

abstract  class sample_abs1 extends sample_abs {

  void abstr_method () {
  }

  void abstr_method1 () {
  }

  void abstr_method2 () {
  }

  void abstr_method3 () {
  }

  public class AbstractClass extends sample_abs1 {

    void abstr_method1 () {
    }
```

```
void abstr_method4 () {
}

public static void main(String[] args) {
  System.out.println("Abstract class demo");
}
}
```

The output will be as follows:

```
Abstract class demo
```

Polymorphism

Polymorphism is the ability of an object to take on many forms. The most common use of polymorphism in OOP occurs when a parent class reference is used to refer to a child class object.

Overloading

Methods with the same names in a class are allowed provided each method has a different signature. Overloading can be done in the following ways:

- Number of arguments
- Type of arguments
- Position of arguments

An example of a Java program with overloading

The following is an example of overloading in a Java program:

```
package MyFirstPackage;

class SampleClass10 {
  void sampleMethod(){
  System.out.println("executing sample method");
}
  void sampleMethod(float b){
    System.out.println("executing sample method" + b);
  }
}

  class SampleClass20 extends SampleClass10 {
    void sampleMethod1(){
```

```
    System.out.println("executing sample method 2");
  }
    void sampleMethod1(int a){
    System.out.println("executing sample method 2" + a);
    }
  }

  public  class OverLoading {
    public static void main(String[] args) {
      SampleClass20 methodcall = new SampleClass20();
      methodcall.sampleMethod1();
      methodcall.sampleMethod();
      methodcall.sampleMethod1(12);
      methodcall.sampleMethod(1);
    }
  }
```

The output will be as follows:

```
executing sample method 2
executing sample method
executing sample method 212
executing sample method1.0
```

Overriding

The subclass accessing the method of a superclass and changing its behavior as per the request of a subclass is called overriding.

An example of a Java program with overriding

The following is an example of overriding in a Java program:

```
package MyFirstPackage;

class SampleClass100 {
  void sampleMethod(){
  System.out.println("executing sample method");
}
  void sampleMethod(float b){
    System.out.println("executing sample method" + b);
  }
  }
```

```
class SampleClass200 extends SampleClass100 {
  void sampleMethod(){
  System.out.println("overidding is done");
}
  void sampleMethod1(int a){
    System.out.println("executing sample method 2" + a);
  }
}

public  class OverRiding {

public static void main(String[] args) {
    SampleClass200 methodcall = new SampleClass200();
    methodcall.sampleMethod();
  }
}
```

The output will be as follows:

`overriding is done`

Encapsulation

Encapsulation is used for protecting the data from the other users accessing the respective class, by marking it as private. The required encapsulated data can be retrieved by using the Java getter and setter methods.

An example of a Java program using encapsulation

The following is an example of encapsulation in a Java program:

```
package MyFirstPackage;

class encap {
  private int salary ;

  public int getI() {
    return salary;
  }

  public void setI(int i) {
    // encap thiExmp = new encap();
    // thiExmp.salary = i * 10;
```

```
      this.salary = i * 10;
    }
  }

  public class encapsulation {
    public static void main(String[] args) {
      encap vara = new encap();
      vara.setI(10);
      System.out.println(vara.getI());
    }
  }
```

The output for the preceding code is as follows:

```
100
```

Constructors

Whenever an instance is created in the method, it is called the constructor of that particular class and is executed by default.

If the user has not written/provided any constructor, the compiler will automatically insert the empty constructor.

A method name similar to its respective class name and method does not return any value.

Overloading is possible but not overriding.

An example of a Java program with a constructor chain

The following is an example of a constructor chain in a Java program:

```
package MyFirstPackage;

class SampleClass4 {
  SampleClass4(){
  System.out.println("executing sample meathod");
}
 }
class SampleClass3 extends SampleClass4 {
  SampleClass3(){
```

```
        System.out.println("executing sample method 2");
    }
  }

public class Constructors {
  public static void main(String[] args) {
    new SampleClass3();
  }
}
```

The output for the preceding code is as follows:

executing sample meathod

executing sample method 2

Interface

All interface classes are by default Public and Abstract, and do not contain any completed methods.

Interface should implement (complete the body of a method) when all the abstract methods are inherited from the superclass (abstract class).

The actual use of interface will be structuring (setting or mandating to set off rules).

An example of a Java program with an interface

The following is an example of an interface in a Java program:

```
package MyFirstPackage;

interface sample_abs2 {
  void abstr_method ();
  void abstr_method1();
}

abstract  class sample_abs3 implements sample_abs2 {
  abstract void abstr_method2 ();

  void abstr_method2A(){
    System.out.println("Abstact class abstr_method2A");
  }
}
```

```
class Interface extends sample_abs3 {//implements is a keyword used to
complete the
//Interface Class
  public void abstr_method () {
    System.out.println("Interface abstr_method implementation");
  }

  public void abstr_method1 () {
    System.out.println("Interface abstr_method1 implementation");
  }

  public void abstr_method2 () {
    System.out.println("Abstact class abstr_method2 implementation");
  }

  public static void main(String[] args) {
    System.out.println("interface class demo");
    Interface objI = new Interface();
    objI.abstr_method();
    objI.abstr_method1();
    objI.abstr_method2();
    objI.abstr_method2A();
  }
}
```

The output will be as follows:

```
interface class demo
Interface abstr_method implementation
Interface abstr_method1 implementation
Abstact class abstr_method2 implementation
Abstact class abstr_method2A
```

Abstract classes compared with interfaces

For more details on abstract classes versus interfaces, visit http://docs.oracle.com/javase/tutorial/java/IandI/abstract.html.

The this keyword

The `this` is a Java keyword that is used as an alternate for creating an instance for a nonstatic variable or method within a same class.

An example for the `this` keyword is as follows:

```
package MyFirstPackage;

class ThisKeyword{
   int id;
   String name;

   //Constructor method
   ThisKeyword(int id, String name){
     //constructor variable and instance variable names are same
     this.id = id;
     this.name = name;
   }

   void display(){
     System.out.println(id + " " + name);
   }

   public static void main(String args[]){
     ThisKeyword objThis1 = new ThisKeyword(1234,"John");
     ThisKeyword objThis2 = new ThisKeyword(2456,"Smith");
     objThis1.display();
     objThis2.display();
   }
}
```

The output for the preceding code will be as follows:

```
1234 John
2456 Smith
```

Data types and variables in Java

The data type specifies the size and type of values that can be stored in an identifier. Variables are the entities that include values and data that act or are acted upon. All variables must have a data type.

Data types

A data type is a classification of data, which can store a specific type of information. Data types are primarily used in computer programming, in which variables are created to store data. Each variable is assigned a data type that determines what type of data the variable may contain.

The term **data type** and **primitive data type** are often used interchangeably.

- **Primitive data type**: Primitive data types are predefined types of data, which are supported by the programming language. For example, `integer`, `character`, and `string` are all primitive data types. Programmers can use these data types when creating variables in their programs. For example, a programmer can create a variable called `lastname` and define it as a `string` data type. The variable will then store data as a string of characters.

- **Non-primitive data type**: These too are used in a programming language, but are instead created by the programmer. They are sometimes called reference variables, or object references, since they reference a memory location, which stores the data. In the Java programming language, non-primitive data types are simply called objects because they are created, rather than predefined. While an object may contain any type of data, the information referenced by the object may still be stored as a primitive data type.

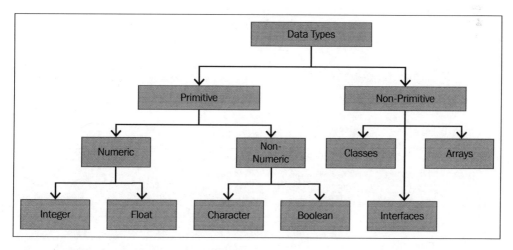

Variables

There are three kinds of variables in Java. They are local variables, instance variables, and class variables, sometimes also known as static variables because the static variable can be used to refer the common property of all objects and the static variable gets memory only once in the class area at the time of class loading.

Local variables

The following are the properties of local variables:

- Local variables are declared in methods, constructors, or blocks
- Local variables are created when the method, constructor, or block is entered and the variable will be destroyed once it exits the method, constructor, or block
- Local variables are visible only within the declared method, constructor, or block
- There is no default value for local variables, so local variables should be declared and an initial value should be assigned before the first use

Here, age is a local variable. This is defined inside the broAge() method and its scope is limited to this method only:

```
package MyFirstPackage;

public class localVariableExample {

  public void broAge(){
    int age = 0;
    age = age + 7;
    System.out.println("My younger brother's age is : " + age);
  }

  public static void main(String args[]){
    localVariableExample localVariableExample = new
localVariableExample();
    localVariableExample.broAge();
  }
}
```

The output will be as follows:

```
My younger brother's age is : 7
```

Instance variables

- Instance variables are declared in a class, but outside a method, constructor or any block.

- When a space is allocated for an object in the heap, a slot for each instance variable value is created.

- Instance variables are created when an object is created with the use of the `new` keyword and destroyed when the object is destroyed.

- Instance variables can be declared in class level before or after use.

- The instance variables are visible for all methods, constructors, and blocks in the class. Normally, it is recommended that you make these variables `private` (access level). However, visibility for subclasses can be given for these variables with the use of access modifiers.

- Instance variables have default values. For numbers, the default value is `0`; for Boolean, it is `false`; and for object references, it is `null`. Values can be assigned during the declaration or within the constructor.

- Instance variables can be accessed directly by calling the variable name inside the class. However, within static methods and different classes, (when instance variables are given accessibility) it should be called using the fully qualified name, `ObjectReference.VariableName`.

The following is an example of instance variables in a Java program:

```
package MyFirstPackage;

public class instanceVariableExample {

  public class Employee{
    // this instance variable is visible for any child class.
    public String name;

    // salary  variable is visible in Employee class only.
    private double salary;

    // The name variable is assigned in the constructor.
    public instanceVariableExample (String empName){
    name = empName;
    }
```

```
   // The salary variable is assigned a value.
   public void setSalary(double empSal){
      salary = empSal;
   }

   // This method prints the employee details.
    public void printEmp(){
       System.out.println("name   : " + name );
       System.out.println("salary :" + salary);
   }

   public static void main(String[] args){
      instanceVariableExample empOne = new instanceVariableExample("Rag
hu");
      empOne.setSalary(1000000);
      empOne.printEmp();
   }
}
```

Output:

```
name   : Raghu
salary :1000000.0
```

Class/static variables

- Class variables, also known as static variables, are declared with the static keyword in a class, but outside a method, constructor or block.
- There will only be one copy of each class variable per class, regardless of how many objects are created from it.
- Static variables are rarely used other than being declared as constants. Constants are variables that are declared as public/private, final, and static. Constant variables never change from their initial value.
- Static variables are stored in static memory. It is rare to use static variables other than declared final and used as either public or private constants.
- Static variables are created when the program starts and destroyed when the program stops.
- Visibility is similar to instance variables. However, most static variables are declared public since they must be available for users of the class.

- Default values are the same as instance variables. For numbers, the default value is 0; for Boolean, it is `false`; and for object references, it is `null`. Values can be assigned during the declaration or within the constructor. Additionally, values can be assigned in special static initializer blocks.
- Static variables can be accessed by calling the class name, `ClassName.VariableName`.
- When declaring class variables as public static final, the variables names (constants) are all in uppercase. If the static variables are not `public` and `final`, the naming syntax is the same as instance and local variables.

The following is an example of class/static variables in a Java program:

```
package MyFirstPackage;

public class classSstaticvariableExample {

  // salary  variable is a private static variable
  private static double salary;

  // DEPARTMENT is a constant
  public static final String DEPT = "Engg ";

  public static void main(String args[]){
    salary = 100000;
    System.out.println(DEPT+"average salary:"+salary);
  }

}
```

The output will be as follows:

```
Engg average salary:100000.0
```

Type casting
The following are the different types of type casting:

Widening
- Extending the data type from smaller to bigger range
- Java allows auto widening

Narrowing

- Decreasing the data type from bigger to smaller range.
- Java doesn't allow auto narrowing, to avoid data loss. You can explicitly perform narrowing.

Example on widening and narrowing

The following is an example for widening and narrowing in a Java program:

```
package MyFirstPackage;

public class Narrowingandwdining {

    public static void main(String[] args) {
        float i = 10 ;
        int j;
        System.out.println(i);

        //double j = 20.89;

        i =  (float) 20.89;
        System.out.println(i);

        j = (int) i;   // can also written as (int) j = (int) i;
        System.out.println(j);
    }
}
```

The output for the preceding code is as follows:

```
10.0
20.89
20
```

Java operators

Operators are special symbols that perform specific operations on *operands*, and then return a result. The following are the operators supported by the Java programming language:

A simple assignment operator

- =: A simple assignment operator

Arithmetic operators

- +: An additive operator (also used for string concatenation)
- -: The subtraction operator
- *: The multiplication operator
- /: The division operator
- %: The remainder operator

Unary operators

- +: Unary plus operator; indicates positive value
- -: Unary minus operator; negates an expression
- ++: Increment operator; increments a value by 1
- --: Decrement operator; decrements a value by 1
- !: Logical complement operator; inverts the value of a Boolean value

Equality and relational operators

- ==: Equals to
- !=: Not equal to
- >: Greater than
- >=: Greater than or equal to
- <: Less than
- <=: Less than or equal to

Conditional operators

- &&: Conditional AND operator
- ||: Conditional OR operator
- ?: Ternary operator

Type comparison operator

- `instanceof`: This compares an object to a specified type

Bitwise and bit shift operators

- `~`: Unary bitwise complement
- `<<`: Signed left shift
- `>>`: Signed right shift
- `>>>`: Unsigned right shift
- `&`: Bitwise AND
- `^`: Bitwise exclusive OR
- `|`: Bitwise inclusive OR

Operator precedence

The operators in the following table are listed according to the precedence order. Operators with higher precedence are evaluated before operators with relatively lower precedence. Operators on the same line have equal precedence.

Precedence	Name	Operators	Associativity
1	postfix	`expr++ expr--`	Right to Left
2	unary	`++expr --expr +expr -expr ~ !`	Right to Left
3	multiplicative	`* / %`	Left to Right
4	additive	`+ -`	Left to Right
5	shift	`<< >> >>>`	Left to Right
6	relational	`< > <= >= instanceof`	Left to Right
7	equality	`== !=`	Left to Right
8	bitwise AND	`&`	Left to Right
9	bitwise exclusive OR	`^`	Left to Right
10	bitwise inclusive OR	`|`	Left to Right
11	logical AND	`&&`	Left to Right
12	logical OR	`||`	Left to Right
13	ternary	`? :`	Right to Left
14	assignment	`= += -= *= /= %= &= ^= |= <<= >>= >>>=`	Right to Left

Reference link for Java operators
```
https://docs.oracle.com/javase/tutorial/java/
nutsandbolts/operators.html
```

Decision and control statements

In Java, decision and control statements allow you to select and execute specific blocks of the code while skipping other sections or statements.

The if statement

The `if` statement consists of a condition followed by one or more statements.

The syntax of an `if` statement is as follows:

```
if(condition)
{
    //Statements will execute if the condition is true
}
```

An example of this is as follows:

```
package MyFirstPackage;
  public class IfCondition {
  public static void main(String[] args) {
    int empSal = 20000;
    if (empSal >= 10000) {
      System.out.println("he is a manager...!");
    }
    else
    {
      System.out.println("he is NOT a manager...!");
    }
  }
}
```

The output of the preceding code is as follows:

```
he is a manager...!
```

The if...else statement

The if statement can be followed by an optional else statement, which executes when the condition is false.

The syntax of an if...else statement is:

```
if(condition){
    //Executes when the condition is true
}else{
    //Executes when the condition is false
}
```

The if...else if...else statement

The if statement can be followed by an optional else if...else statement, which is very useful to test various conditions using single if...else if statement.

The syntax of an if...else statement is:

```
if(condition 1){
   //Executes when the condition 1 is true
}else if(condition 2){
   //Executes when the condition 2 is true
}else if(condition 3){
   //Executes when the condition 3 is true
}else {
   //Executes when the one of the above condition is true.
}
```

The nested if...else statement

It is always legal to nest if..else statements. When using if...else if... else... statements, there are a few points to keep in mind:

- An if statement can have zero or one else statement and it must come after any else if statements

- An if statement can have zero to many else if statements and they must come before the else statement

- Once an else if statement succeeds, none of the remaining else if statements or else statements will be tested

The syntax for a nested `if...else` statement is as follows:

```
if(condition 1){
  //Executes when the condition 1 is true
  if(condition 2){
    //Executes when the condition 2 is true
  }
}
```

The switch statement

A `switch` statement allows a variable to be tested for equality against a list of values. Each value is called a `case`, and the variable being switched on is checked for each `case`.

The syntax of a switch statement is:

```
switch(expression){
case value :
//Statements
break; //optional
case value :
//Statements
break; //optional
//You can have any number of case statements.
default : //Optional
//Statements
}
```

Loops

The following are the different types of loops in Java:

The while loop

A `while` loop is a control structure that allows you to repeat a task a certain number of times.

The syntax of a `while` loop is:

```
While(condition){
  //statements;
}
```

The do...while loop

A do...while loop is similar to a while loop, except that a do...while loop is guaranteed to execute at least once.

The syntax of a do...while loop is as follows:

```
do {
  //statements;
} while(condition);
```

The for loop

A for loop is a repetition control structure that allows you to efficiently write a loop that needs to execute a specific number of times. A for loop is useful when you know how many times a task is to be repeated.

The syntax of a for loop is as follows:

```
for(initialization; condition; update)
{
  //statements;
}
```

An example of a for loop is as follows:

```
package MyFirstPackage;
public class Loop {
  public static void main(String[] args) {
    for (int i = 0 ; i <= 10 ; i ++ ){
      System.out.println(i);
    }
  }
}
```

The output for the preceding code is as follows:

```
0
1
2
3
4
5
6
7
```

8

9

10

The for each loop in Java

As of **Java 5,** the for each loop was introduced. This loop is mainly used for arrays iteration.

The syntax of the for each loop is as follows:

```
for(declaration : expression)
{
   //statements;
}
```

The break keyword

* The break keyword is used to exit from the entire loop
* The break keyword must be used inside any of the loops or a switch statement
* The break keyword will stop the execution of the innermost loop and start executing the next line of code after the block

The continue keyword

* The continue keyword can be used in any of the loop controls. It causes the loop to immediately jump to the next iteration of the loop

String class functions

The following are the most commonly used functions of the String class:

The charAt() function

The following line of code is an example of the charAt() function in a Java program:

```
public char charAt(int index)
```

The `charAt()` function returns the char value at the specified index. An index ranges from 0 to `length()` - 1. The first `char` value of the sequence is at index 0, the next at index 1, and so on, as for array indexing. The following is another example:

```
String str = "welcome";
System.out.println(str.charAt(2));
```

The output is displayed here:

```
l
```

The equalsIgnoreCase() function

The following line of code is an example of the `equalsIgnoreCase()` function in a Java program. It compares one `String` to another `String`, ignoring case considerations. Two strings are considered equal ignoring case if they are of the same length, and corresponding characters in the two strings are equal ignoring case.

```
String str = "java";
System.out.println(str.equalsIgnoreCase("JAVA"));
```

The output will be as follows:

```
true
```

The length() function

The following line of code is an example of the `length*()` function in a Java program:

```
public int length()
```

The `length()` function returns the length of this string. The length is equal to the number of Unicode code units in the string:

```
String str = "Welcome";
System.out.println(str.length());
```

The output will be as follows:

```
7
```

The replace() function

The following line of code is an example of the `replace()` function in a Java program:

```
public String replaceAll(String regex, String replacement)
```

The `replace()` function returns a new string resulting from replacing all occurrences of `oldChar` in this string with `newChar`:

```
String str = "Java programming";
System.out.println(str.replace('p','P'));
```

The output will be as follows:

```
Java Programming
```

The substring() function

The following line of code is an example of the `substring()` function in a Java program:

```
public String substring(int beginIndex)
```

The `substring()` function returns a new string that is a substring of this string. The substring begins with the character at the specified index and extends to the end of this string:

```
String str = "Java Programming";
System.out.println(str.substring(5));
```

The output will be as follows:

```
Programming
```

The following line of code is another example of the `substring()` function in a Java program:

```
public String substring(int beginIndex, int endIndex)
```

This returns a new string that is a substring of this string. The substring begins at the specified `beginIndex` and extends to the character at the index `endIndex - 1`. Thus, the length of the substring is `endIndex-beginIndex`:

```
String str = "Java Programming";
System.out.println(str.substring(5,11));
```

The output will be as follows:

```
Program
```

The toLowerCase() function

The following line of code is an example of the `toLowerCase()` function in a Java program:

```
public String toLowerCase()
```

The `toLowerCase()` function converts all of the characters in this `String` to lowercase using the rules of the default locale:

```
String str = "JAVA";
System.out.println(str.toLowerCase());
```

The output will be as follows:

```
java
```

The toUpperCase() function

The following line of code is an example of the `toUpperCase()` function in a Java program:

```
public String toUpperCase()
```

The `toUpperCase()` function converts all of the characters in this `String` to uppercase using the rules of the default locale:

```
String str = "java";
System.out.println(str.toUpperCase());
```

The output will be as follows:

```
JAVA
```

The trim() function

The following line of code is an example of the `trim()` function in a Java program:

```
public String trim()
```

The `trim()` function returns a copy of the string, with leading and trailing whitespace omitted. This method can be used to trim whitespace from the beginning and end of a string:

```
String str = "   Java   ";
System.out.println(str.trim());
```

The output will be as follows:

```
Java
```

Following is a link on more information on String class methods:
https://docs.oracle.com/javase/6/docs/api/java/lang/String.html

Collections

A *collection* is simply an object that groups multiple elements into a single unit. Collections are used to store, retrieve, manipulate, and communicate aggregate data. Typically, they represent data items that form a natural group, such as a poker hand (a collection of cards), a mail folder (a collection of letters), or a telephone directory (a mapping of names to phone numbers).

What is a Collections framework?

A collections framework is a unified architecture for representing and manipulating groups of data as a single unit collection. All collections frameworks consist of the following parts:

- Interfaces: The Java collections framework interface provides the abstract data type to represent a collection. The root interface of Collections framework hierarchy is `java.util.Collection`. Some other important interfaces are `java.util.List` and `java.util.Set`. All the collections framework interfaces are present in the `java.util` package.

- Implementations: These are the core implementations of the collection interfaces. They are reusable data structures to create different types of collections. Some important collection classes are `ArrayList`, `LinkedList`, `HashSet`, and `TreeSet`.

- Algorithms: These are the methods that perform useful and reusable common functionalities, such as searching and sorting, on objects that implement collection interfaces. The same method can be used on many different implementations of the appropriate collection interface.

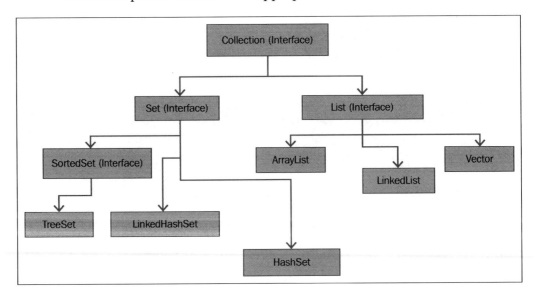

The following list describes the core collection interfaces:

- The **Collection** interface is the root of the collection hierarchy. A collection represents a group of objects known as its elements. The Collection interface is the least common denominator that all collections implement and is used to pass collections around and to manipulate them when maximum generality is desired. Some types of collections allow duplicate elements, and others do not. Some are ordered and others are unordered. The Java platform doesn't provide any direct implementations of this interface but provides implementations of more specific sub-interfaces, such as Set and List.

- The **Set** interface is a collection that cannot contain duplicate elements. This interface models the mathematical set abstraction and is used to represent sets, such as the cards comprising a poker hand, the courses making up a student's schedule, or the processes running on a machine.

 For more information, please go through http://docs.oracle. com/javase/tutorial/collections/intro/.

Following is an example code on Collections:

```java
import java.util.HashSet;
import java.util.Iterator;
import java.util.Set;

public class SetCollection {
  public static void main(String args[]) {
    //Create a set
    Set<String> uniqueSet = new HashSet<String>();
    // Add an elements to set
    uniqueSet.add("Apple");
    uniqueSet.add("Cat");
    uniqueSet.add("Apple");
    uniqueSet.add("Ball");

    //Print an elements of the Set
    System.out.println("UniqueSet: " + uniqueSet);

    //Retrieve element from set using Iterator
    Iterator<String> iterator = uniqueSet.iterator();
    while (iterator.hasNext()) {
      System.out.println("Iterator: " + iterator.next());
    }
  }
}
```

The output will be as follows:

```
UniqueSet: [Ball, Cat, Apple]
Iterator: Ball
Iterator: Cat
Iterator: Apple
```

- **List**: This is an ordered collection (sometimes called a sequence). Lists can contain duplicate elements. The user of a list generally has precise control over where in the list each element is inserted and can access elements by their integer index (position). The following is an example of code on lists:

```java
import java.util.ArrayList;
import java.util.Iterator;
import java.util.List;

public class ListCollection {
  public static void main(String args[]) {
    //Create a List
```

```
        List<String> list = new ArrayList<String>();
        // Add an elements to List
        list.add("Apple");
        list.add("Cat");
        list.add("Apple");
        list.add("Ball");

        //Print an elements of the List
        System.out.println("List: " + list);

        //Retrieve element from list using Iterator
        Iterator<String> iterator = list.iterator();
        while (iterator.hasNext()) {
          System.out.println("Iterator: " + iterator.next());
        }
    }
}
```

The output will be as follows:

```
List: [Apple, Cat, Apple, Ball]
Iterator: Apple
Iterator: Cat
Iterator: Apple
Iterator: Ball
```

- **SortedSet**: This is a set that maintains its elements in an ascending order. Several additional operations are provided to take advantage of the ordering. Sorted sets are used for naturally ordered sets, such as word lists and membership rolls. The following is an example of SortedSet:

```
import java.util.Iterator;
import java.util.SortedSet;
import java.util.TreeSet;

public class SortedSetCollection {
  public static void main(String args[]) {
    //Create a set
    SortedSet<String> sortSet = new TreeSet<String>();
    // Add an elements to set
    sortSet.add("Apple");
    sortSet.add("Cat");
    sortSet.add("Apple");
    sortSet.add("Ball");
```

```
//Print an elements of the Set
System.out.println("UniqueSet: " + sortSet);

//Retrieve element from set using Iterator
Iterator<String> iterator = sortSet.iterator();
while (iterator.hasNext()) {
  System.out.println("Iterator: " + iterator.next());
}
  }
}
```

The output will be as follows:

```
SortedSet: [Apple, Ball, Cat]
Iterator: Apple
Iterator: Ball
Iterator: Cat
```

 Following is a reference link for the Collection framework:
`http://docs.oracle.com/javase/tutorial/`
`collections/intro/`

Exception handling

An *exception* is an event, which occurs during the execution of a program, that disrupts the normal flow of the program's instructions.

Types of exceptions

- Checked exception
- Error
- Runtime exception

1. Checked exceptions are checked at compile time. If a code throws a checked exception, then the associated block or method must handle the exception. For example, FileNotFoundException is a checked exception. If a method creates the FileInputStream object to read data from, a file must handle FileNotFoundException. If the specified file does not exist, then FileNotFoundException occurs and this exception must be caught or thrown.

2. Errors are exceptional conditions that are external to the application and it's not possible to anticipate and recover from them, for example, hardware failure, stack overflow error, and out of memory error. These errors should not be handled.

3. Runtime exceptions are unchecked exceptions and these exceptions are not checked at compile time. Runtime exceptions can occur anywhere in a program, and throw `RuntimeException` when the user calls a method incorrectly. For example, in a method, if an argument is null, then a method might throw `NullPointerException`, which is an unchecked exception. `ArrayIndexOutOfBoundsException` is another example of a runtime exception. Errors and runtime exceptions are collectively known as unchecked exceptions.

Exception handler components

Components of exception handler are `try`, `catch`, and `finally` blocks, as shown in the figure that follows:

```
try {

} catch (ExceptionType name) {

} catch (ExceptionType name) {

} finally {

}
```

The first step in constructing an exception handler is to enclose the code that might throw an exception within a `try` block. You associate exception handlers with a `try` block by providing one or more `catch` blocks directly after the `try` block. No code can be between the end of the `try` block and the beginning of the first `catch` block.

Each `catch` block is an exception handler that handles the type of exception indicated by its argument. The argument type, `ExceptionType`, declares the type of exception that the handler can handle and must be the name of a class that inherits from the `Throwable` class. The handler can refer to the exception with `name`. The `catch` block contains code that is executed if and when the exception handler is invoked. The runtime system invokes the exception handler when the handler is the first one in the call stack whose `ExceptionType` matches the type of the exception thrown. The system considers it a match if the thrown object can legally be assigned to the exception handler's argument.

The `finally` block always executes when the `try` block exits. This ensures that the `finally` block is executed even if an unexpected exception occurs. However, `finally` is useful for more than just exception handling; it allows the programmer to avoid having cleanup code accidentally bypassed by a `return`, `continue`, or `break`. Putting cleanup code in a `finally` block is always a good practice, even when no exceptions are anticipated.

An example for exception handler components are as follows:

```
public class ExceptionHandlingExample {

    public static void main(String args[]){
    try{
      //code that might throw an exception in try block
      System.out.println("Try block executing...");
      int i = 10/0;
      System.out.println(i);
    }
    catch(ArithmeticException e){
      //handles ArithmeticException
      System.out.println("Arithmetic Exception catch block
executing...");
      System.out.println(e);
    }
    catch(NullPointerException e){
      //handles NullPointerException
      System.out.println("Null Pointer Exception catch block
executing...");
      System.out.println(e);
    }
    finally{
      System.out.println("finally block is always executed");
    }
    }
}
```

The output is as follows:

```
Try block executing...
Arithmetic Exception catch block executing...
java.lang.ArithmeticException: / by zero
finally block is always executed
```

The throw keyword

The `throw` keyword is used to explicitly throw an exception. We can throw either checked or unchecked exceptions. The throw keyword is mainly used to throw a custom exception.

The following example performs division operation by passing two integer numbers as a parameter. If the denominator is zero, then throw `ArithmeticException`; otherwise, calculate the division operation:

```java
public class ThrowExample {

    private int calculateDivision(int number1, int number2){
      if(number2 == 0){
    //throw exception
      throw new ArithmeticException("Division not possible, denominator
should be greater than zero.");
      } else{
        //calculate division and return result
        return number1/number2;
        }
    }

    public static void main(String args[]){
        try {
        ThrowExample obj = new ThrowExample();
        //call calculateDivision method
        System.out.println(obj.calculateDivision(10, 0));
      } catch (Exception e) {
        //if any exception catch and print the message
        System.out.println(e.getMessage());
        }
      }
    }
```

The output will be as follows:

```
Division not possible, denominator should be greater than zero.
```

 Refer to the following reference to learn more about exception handling:
https://docs.oracle.com/javase/tutorial/essential/exceptions/index.html

Java IO

Java IO is an API used for reading from a file and writing data to a file known as Java input and output operations. The File class in the Java IO API gives access to the underlying filesystem. Using the File class, you can perform the following operations:

- Check if a file or directory exists
- Create a directory if it does not exist
- Read the length of a file
- Rename or move a file
- Delete a file
- Check if the path is a file or directory
- Read the list of files in a directory

The File class gives access to the file and file system metadata. To perform read and write operations on a file, you should use FileInputStream and FileOutputStream. FileInputStream and FileOutputStream classes are used to read and write data in a file.

The FileOutputStream class

A FileOutputStream class is an output stream for writing data to a File or to a FileDescriptor. Whether or not a file is available or may be created, depends upon the underlying platform. Some platforms, in particular, allow a file to be opened for writing by only one FileOutputStream (or other file-writing object) at a time. In such situations, the constructors in this class will fail if the file involved is already open. FileOutputStream is meant for writing streams of raw bytes such as image data. For writing streams of characters, consider using FileWriter.

The FileInputStream class

A FileInputStream class obtains input bytes from a file in a filesystem. What files are available depends on the host environment. FileInputStream is meant for reading streams of raw bytes such as image data. For reading streams of characters, consider using FileReader.

The following example shows that `FileOutputStream` writes the String contents as a stream of bytes into a file called `contents.txt`. The `FileInputStream` class makes it possible to read the contents of a file as a stream of bytes:

```java
import java.io.FileInputStream;
import java.io.FileOutputStream;

public class FileIOStreamExample{
   public static void main(String args[]){
   try{
      //FileOutputStream create file and connect write mode
      FileOutputStream fOut = new FileOutputStream("c:\\abc.txt");
      String str = "Working with Java FileInputStream and
FileOutputStream class";

      //Contents of bytes and write to a file
      byte stringBytes[]=str.getBytes();
      fOut.write(stringBytes);

      //Close the file
      fOut.close();
      System.out.println("Written contents to file...");

      //FileinputStraem connect read mode
      FileInputStream fIn = new FileInputStream("c:\\abc.txt");
      int i;
      while((i = fIn.read())!= -1){
      System.out.print((char)i);
      }

      //Close the file
      fIn.close();
      System.out.println();
      System.out.println("Read contents from file...");
   }catch(Exception e){
      System.out.println(e);
      }
   }
}
```

The output will be as follows:

```
Written contents to file...
Working with Java FileInputStream and FileOutputStream class
Read contents from file...
```

Java coding standards

This section explains us on the importance of coding standards and why they are required.

Why are coding standards required?

Coding standards for Java are very important and play a major role in software development because they lead to a better consistency within the code of all developers. In turn, consistency leads other users to understand code easily, and makes it easier to develop, and maintain. Code that is difficult to understand and maintain leads the high risk of being scrapped and rewritten from scratch.

To know about coding standards refer to the following link:
`http://www.oracle.com/technetwork/java/javase/`
`documentation/codeconventions-139411.html#16711`

Summary

The following table summarizes the various types of topics we covered in this chapter:

Packages, classes and objects	
Java sample program	
OOPs concepts	Inheritance
	Abstraction / Abstract Class
	Polymorphism (Overriding, Overloading)
	Encapsulation
	Constructor
	Interface
Data types and variables in Java	
Data type conversions	Type Casting
Operators	Arithmetic operators
	Relational or comparison operators
	Logical operators
	Concatenation operators
	Assignment operators
	Operator Precedence

Decision and control statements	If...else
	If...else if...else
	If...else If...else if...else
	Switch case
	Nested If
Loops	For loop
	Nested for loop
	Exit for
	Do while loops (optional)
	do_loop...while (optional)
	For...each...next (optional)
	While...wend (optional)
String functions	Split_function
	Ucase
	Lcase
	len
	right
	left
	mid
	trim, rtrim, ltrim
Collections	
Exception handling	Try...catch
Coding standards	
File IO	Usage of file IO
	Reading and writing a file
	Handling logs and property files

Self-test Questions

1. Classes belong to which data type?

    a. Primitive

    b. Non-primitive

    c. Both a and b

    d. None

2. Which one of the following is true for local variables?

    a. Local variables are declared in methods, constructors, or blocks

    b. Local variables are declared in a class, but outside a method, constructor or any block

    c. Both a and b

    d. None

B
Answers for Self-test Questions

Chapter 1

1. **Answer:** c.
2. **Answer:** b.
3. **Answer:** a.
4. **Answer:** Verify allows a test to continue and keep track of all verify errors. Assert will stop a test immediately when the assert fails.
5. **Answer:** b.
6. **Answer:** a.
7. **Answer:** Click on the button with the arrow and three solid green lines.

Chapter 2

1. **Answer:** d.
2. **Answer:** c.
3. **Answer:** a and b.
4. **Answer:** a.
5. **Answer:** `//input/following-sibling::input`.
6. **Answer:** `css=input + input`.

Chapter 3

1. **Answer**: a.

2. **Answer**: a.

3. **Answer**: a.

4. **Answer**: b.

5. **Answer**: a.

Chapter 4

1. **Answer**: b.

2. **Answer**: b.

3. **Answer**: It will not throw any exception, instead it will return 0 when elements are not found, since it's a collection list.

4. **Answer**: Implicit wait is applied globally to all the elements throughout the execution, while explicit wait can be applied to a specific web element.

Chapter 5

1. **Answer**: The Page Object design pattern gives us a way to abstract our tests away so that we can make these tests more maintainable. We can make tests that only require updating if new steps have been added; otherwise, it just requires the page object to be updated.

2. **Answer**: `@FindBy(how=How.ID, using='myId')`.

3. **Answer**: `@CacheLookup`.

4. **Answer**: `PageFactory.initElements();`.

Chapter 6

1. **Answer**: Create a profile object and call the `setPreference()` method with the needed details.

2. **Answer**: We can use the `FirefoxBinary` class to tell it where to look.

3. **Answer**: ChromeOptions.

4. **Answer**: The **PATH** environment variable needs to be set with where the ChromeDriver executable lives. This is so that when we call ChromeDriver with our Java code, it will load the relevant executable and load the browser as quickly as possible.

5. **Answer**: Use the latest stable version of Opera.

6. **Answer**: Use the `OperaProfile` object and update the preferences where needed.

7. **Answer**: All versions of IE6, IE7, IE8, and IE9 for both 32-bit and 64-bit installations.

Chapter 7

1. **Answer**: c.

2. **Answer**: c.

3. **Answer**: b.

4. **Answer**: b.

5. **Answer**: a.

6. **Answer**: a.

Chapter 8

1. **Answer**: `./android create avd -n my_android -t 14 -c 100M`.

2. **Answer**: a.

3. **Answer**: c.

4. **Answer**: `adb -s <serialId> shell am start -a android.intent.action.MAIN -n org.openqa.selenium.android.app/.MainActivity`.

5. **Answer**: c.

Chapter 9

1. **Answer**: `java -jar selenium-server.jar -role hub`.

2. **Answer**: `http://nameofmachine:4444/grid/console`, where `nameofmachine` is the name of the machine that is running the hub. If it is on the same machine as you are currently on, put `localhost` or `127.0.0.1`.

3. **Answer**: `port 4444`.

4. **Answer**: `-browser browserName="internet explorer"`, `maxInstances=1`, `platform=WINDOWS`.

Chapter 10

1. **Answer:** `Action`.
2. **Answer:** `build()`.
3. **Answer:** `Perform()`.
4. **Answer.** `moveByOffset()`.

Chapter 11

1. **Answer:** c.
2. **Answer:** b.

Chapter 12

1. **Answer:** c.
2. **Answer:** Base64.
3. **Answer:** X11 Virtual Frame Buffer.
4. **Answer:** `-screen`.
5. **Answer:** HTTP Archive or HAR.
6. **Answer:** `newHar()`.

Chapter 13

1. **Answer:** Create a new instance of the browser you want to use using Selenium WebDriver. Then pass this into the `WebDriverBackedSelenium` with the URL. This you would like to test. It will look like this:

```
@Before
  public void setup(){
     driver = new FirefoxDriver();
     selenium = new WebDriverBackedSelenium(driver,
      http://book.theautomatedtester.co.uk
```

Appendix A

1. **Answer:** b.
2. **Answer:** a.

Index

D

data driven approach, Test Automation Frameworks Evolution
about 146
advantages 146
disadvantages 146
Data Engine 150
data type
about 249
non-primitive data type 249
primitive data type 249
decision and control statements
about 257
if...else if...else statement 258
if...else statement 258
if statement 257
nested if...else statement 258
switch statement 259
defaults
Selenium server, adding with 191, 192
design pattern 109
developer account, Apple
URL 179
direct XPath
elements, finding by 54
using, in test 54
do...while loop 260
DOM (Document Object Model) 8
driver 85
Driver Engine
about 150
Config Engine 150
Data Engine 150
Page Object Handler 150
DSL (Domain-specific language) 109

E

Eclipse
downloading 79
installing, on Windows 79
URL, for downloading 72
WebDriver, configuring with 80
Eclipse IDE 149
Eclipse IDE, for Java EE Developers Edition
URL, for downloading 79

Eclipse IDE, with Java project
setting up, for TestNG 78
setting up, for WebDriver 78
Eclipse workspace
sample Java project, importing in 239
element attributes
using, in XPath queries 56
element existence
finding, without throwing an error 102
element, finding
by inner text 66
by partial text 66
by text 57
child nodes used 61
sibling nodes used 62
element, finding on page by ClassName
findElementByClassName()
method used 92, 93
element, finding on page by ID
findElementById() method used 87, 88
element, finding on page by link text
findElementByLinkText()
method used 98, 99
element, finding on page by name
findElementByName() method used 89, 90
element, finding on page by XPath
findElementByXPath() method used 95, 96
element IDs
using, in CSS selectors 63
element, moving
to offset 203
with drag and drop by offset 203, 204
elements
locating, by ID 47
moving, on page 49
working with 63
XPath axis, leveraging with 57
elements, finding
about 86
by accessing DOM via JavaScript 52
by attributes 64
by CSS 60, 61
by direct XPath 54
by ID 48, 49
by link text 51, 52
by name 50

W

WebDriver
  configuring, with Eclipse 80
WebDriver API
  about 74
  URL 74
WebDriver architecture
  about 73
  JSON Wire Protocol 74
  Selenium server 75
  WebDriver API 74
  WebDriver SPI 74
WebDriverBackedSelenium
  about 233, 234
  used, for converting tests to Selenium
      WebDriver 234-236
WebDriver JAR files
  downloading 78
WebDriver SPI 74
WebStorage
  local storage 217
  session storage 219
  working with 217
while loop 259
widening, type casting
  about 253
  example 254
windows
  multiplying 21
WYSIWYG editor 203

X

X11 Virtual Frame Buffer. *See* **XVFB**
XPath
  elements, finding by 53
  used, for finding nth element of type 54, 55
XPath axis
  leveraging, with elements 57
  using 57-59
  working with 59
XPath queries
  element attributes, using in 56
XVFB
  server, setting up 227
  tests, running in 227, 228
  URL, for setting up 227
  using, with Selenium 226

Y

YAML file
  Selenium Grid 1, using with 194, 195

Thank you for buying
Learning Selenium Testing Tools
Third Edition

About Packt Publishing

Packt, pronounced 'packed', published its first book, *Mastering phpMyAdmin for Effective MySQL Management*, in April 2004, and subsequently continued to specialize in publishing highly focused books on specific technologies and solutions.

Our books and publications share the experiences of your fellow IT professionals in adapting and customizing today's systems, applications, and frameworks. Our solution-based books give you the knowledge and power to customize the software and technologies you're using to get the job done. Packt books are more specific and less general than the IT books you have seen in the past. Our unique business model allows us to bring you more focused information, giving you more of what you need to know, and less of what you don't.

Packt is a modern yet unique publishing company that focuses on producing quality, cutting-edge books for communities of developers, administrators, and newbies alike. For more information, please visit our website at www.packtpub.com.

About Packt Open Source

In 2010, Packt launched two new brands, Packt Open Source and Packt Enterprise, in order to continue its focus on specialization. This book is part of the Packt Open Source brand, home to books published on software built around open source licenses, and offering information to anybody from advanced developers to budding web designers. The Open Source brand also runs Packt's Open Source Royalty Scheme, by which Packt gives a royalty to each open source project about whose software a book is sold.

Writing for Packt

We welcome all inquiries from people who are interested in authoring. Book proposals should be sent to author@packtpub.com. If your book idea is still at an early stage and you would like to discuss it first before writing a formal book proposal, then please contact us; one of our commissioning editors will get in touch with you.

We're not just looking for published authors; if you have strong technical skills but no writing experience, our experienced editors can help you develop a writing career, or simply get some additional reward for your expertise.

open source
community experience distilled

Selenium WebDriver Practical Guide

ISBN: 978-1-78216-885-0   Paperback: 264 pages

Interactively automate web applications using Selenium WebDriver

1. Covers basic to advanced concepts of WebDriver.

2. Learn how to design a more effective automation framework.

3. Explores all of the APIs within WebDriver.

4. Acquire an in-depth understanding of each concept through practical code examples.

Selenium Design Patterns and Best Practices

ISBN: 978-1-78398-270-7   Paperback: 270 pages

Build a powerful, stable, and automated test suite using Selenium WebDriver

1. Keep up with the changing pace of your web application by creating an agile test suite.

2. Save time and money by making your Selenium tests 99% reliable.

3. Improve the stability of your test suite and your programing skills by following a step-by-step continuous improvement tutorial.

Please check **www.PacktPub.com** for information on our titles

PUBLISHING

Selenium Testing Tools Cookbook

ISBN: 978-1-84951-574-0   Paperback: 326 pages

Over 90 recipes to build, maintain, and improve test automation with Selenium WebDriver

1. Learn to leverage the power of Selenium WebDriver with simple examples that illustrate real world problems and their workarounds.

2. Each sample demonstrates key concepts allowing you to advance your knowledge of Selenium WebDriver in a practical and incremental way.

3. Explains testing of mobile web applications with Selenium Drivers for platforms such as iOS and Android.

Learning Selenium Testing Tools with Python

ISBN: 978-1-78398-350-6   Paperback: 216 pages

A practical guide on automated web testing with Selenium using Python

1. Write and automate tests for your applications with Selenium.

2. Explore the Selenium WebDriver API for easy implementations of small to complex operations on browsers and web applications.

3. Packed with easy and practical examples that get you started with Selenium WebDriver.

Please check **www.PacktPub.com** for information on our titles

24405142R00180

Made in the USA
San Bernardino, CA
24 September 2015